RIDING LOGIC

RIDING LOGIC

BY

WILHELM MÜSELER

Translated from the German by

F. W. SCHILLER

WITH 64 ILLUSTRATIONS

KEN KIMBEL
P.O. Box 1288
Plant City Florida

First published in Germany as Müseler: REITLEHRE
By Paul Parey Verlag
Berlin & Hamburg

This translation first published in Great Britain
June 17th 1937
Reprinted three times
Reprinted 1961
Third edition 1965

First published in the United States of America 1962
Revised edition 1965

Printed in Great Britain

TRANSLATOR'S PREFACE

WHEN the late Lt.-Col. M. F. McTaggart suggested an English translation of this book he did not realize that it would be the last active step he would be able to take in the interests of the English-speaking riding public. A tribute is due to this game little man who devoted almost a lifetime to preaching the wisdom of horsemanship. No matter how little personal success he may have won in the show ring or on the race-course, no matter how much opinions about his ideas and methods may differ: it will be universally agreed that he was a true horseman in the best sense of the word. He had but one great ideal at heart: to improve the general standard of English riding. Loving his country and his fellow-sportsmen, he wanted to see British riders in the front ranks; and when he criticized them, he did so openly and unhesitatingly, and not because he wanted to find fault but because he wanted to help.

It was in this spirit that he suggested to me that the excellent German book *Reitlehre* should be made accessible to the English-speaking public. This book describes in plain, sober language the methods by which the rider is taught to control his horse and the horse to let himself be controlled. It begins with the elements and proceeds to the stage at which man and mount, having gone through a course of 'School Riding', are ready to 'specialize', as it were, in one or other particular branch of the art of riding—Show Riding, Jumping, Haute École or just plain, simple Hacking.

Unfortunately, there seems to be some misapprehension amongst English riders as to the nature of 'School Riding'. More often than not it is confounded with 'Haute École';

some even go so far as to call it 'trick riding'. It is nothing of the sort. Ordinary 'School Riding' is the fundamental education of both rider and horse; it is, if I may be allowed to coin a phrase, the Grammar School for man and mount alike, and it is regarded as such by practically every Continental horseman, no matter what his particular individual 'horsey' creed. There are even trainers of racehorses, especially hurdlers and steeplechasers, who take their pupils regularly to school (it need not always be a covered one) during the off-season, to make them 'handy' and obedient, or to break them of bad habits, such as rushing their fences, storming away, being difficult to turn, etc. Ordinary School Riding comprises all forward movements in the three gaits, all turns and side-steps and the rein-back, as well as all those 'exercises' and 'lessons' which help to develop suppleness and complete obedience in the horse.

'Haute École', on the other hand—which is strictly distinct from 'Circus Riding' or 'Trick Riding' (this is where the word comes in)—teaches all those highly 'collected' movements which any horse, particularly the proud stallion, can, and actually does, execute when in a state of excitement at liberty, such as the Salute (with one foreleg raised), the Passage, the Spanish Trot, the Pesade, and even the Ballotade (fighting stallions). Certain dance steps or other artificial movements belong to another branch of animal training and have nothing to do with 'Haute École'.

School Riding, as treated in this book, is therefore nothing but a means to establishing perfect understanding and harmony between man and mount; it lays the foundation for all further work, no matter what its nature. For this reason the author wants it to be understood that 'School Riding' need not be an end in itself. For this reason he also maintains that a rider can never be a really proficient HORSEMAN unless he practises regularly three things: *school riding, cross-country riding,* and *jumping.*

When I undertook to translate this book I knew it would not be an easy task. 'The book describes foreign methods and contains a number of *termini technici,* for which the English language has no fitting synonyms. In view of the purely technical nature of the work I have endeavoured to adhere as closely as possible to the author's own wording. Consequently I have had to resort to expressions, some of which may sound unfamiliar. Many of the short 'commands' and business-like exclamations, for example, I have had to circumscribe, for the simple reason that the action itself, or the manner of its execution, or the method of its teaching, is not part of the English sportsman's vocabulary. In most Continental countries the source of all riding knowledge is the Army, the influence of which upon the sport is predominant. It is therefore natural that in these countries most civilian riders are familiar with the cavalryman's methods and vocabulary.

There is in particular one 'action', well known to every Continental horseman, to which I want to draw the reader's attention, because it is of supreme importance for all school work and because there is no adequate English expression for it. In German it is called *das Kreuz anziehen* and it relates to a certain action of the back and its muscles. Although it really concerns more the loins and the small of the back than the actual back or spinal column, I have ventured to use the terms 'back', 'back-muscle action' and 'bracing the back' throughout the following pages, in the hope that these expressions will eventually form an indispensable part of every horseman's and horsewoman's vocabulary. The action itself is thoroughly described in the sections entitled, 'Following the Movement of the Horse' and 'Bracing the Back', and its importance cannot be emphasized too much or too often.

Another unfamiliar expression is 'showing the horse the way to the ground', derived from the German *dem Pferde den Weg in die Tiefe zeigen*. This subject was mentioned by Lt.-Col. McTaggart in one of his earlier books, but unfortunately he only quotes the German and does not give any translation of it. By 'showing the horse the way to the ground' we do not want to teach him how to 'peck' or to come down on his nose ! The phrase describes the method by which a horse is taught to stretch his neck and to find the bit, so that he can ultimately be 'taken up' and 'collected'. This sounds a little weird, but let Major Müseler explain it to you. He does it magnificently and convincingly, for his is the knowledge that master hands down to master, and the experience that can only be acquired by a life-long association with nature's noblest animal—the horse.

One more small piece of advice: be patient, fair reader ! 'Patience' should be written across your stable door, across the four walls of your riding school, across the pommel of your saddle. Be patient in reading this book and still more so in applying its teachings. They are expressed in plain simple words. They may perhaps lack the mysterious ''ossy' language, this cherished treasure of the initiated, but they will soon raise you from the condition of being carried about by a horse to HORSEMANSHIP and HORSEMASTERSHIP, and riding will be a pleasure instead of a 'bally nuisance'.

Good Luck and—

        ''ustle your 'osses and 'arden your 'earts !'

London, *January 1937*   F. W. S.

AUTHOR'S PREFACE

ANYBODY CAN LEARN TO RIDE, for riding is nothing but skill. Skill can only be acquired by continual 'trying out' and practice, but not by imitation of a model. Once skill has been acquired, however, it should be exercised in 'good form'.

Riding is pleasant and can be made an art. And who would not be an artist? Only those, however, who try with their whole soul, to understand the horse's psychic disposition and who endeavour to establish perfect harmony by sensitive feel instead of crude force, are entitled to be called artists. 'Feel' is no 'black magic', and anybody can acquire it to a considerable degree.

The end of all schooling and dressage is perfect harmony between man and mount—Beauty. The horse must show that he feels comfortable and the rider must not betray how hard it is to achieve this!

W. MÜSELER

THE RIDER SHOULD PRACTISE REGULARLY
THE FOLLOWING THREE THINGS :

RIDING IN THE SCHOOL.

RIDING ACROSS COUNTRY (*see* p. 155).

JUMPING (*see* p. 159).

A RIDER WHO BELITTLES OR NEGLECTS ANY
ONE OF THESE THREE WILL NEVER FULLY
MASTER HIS HORSE.

Most of the illustrations in this book are arranged in series,
so that the reader can train his eye and increase his understanding by comparison.

CONTENTS

I

THE TRAINING OF THE RIDER

II

THE SCHOOLING OF THE HORSE

THE PURPOSE OF SCHOOLING   57

PRINCIPAL VIEWS ON DRESSAGE   60

THE PROCEDURE IN SCHOOL WORK   62

FIRST STAGE OF SCHOOLING   63

    Making the Green Horse Used to the Rider's
        Weight   63

SECOND STAGE OF SCHOOLING   65

    To 'Put the Horse to the Aids'   65

        What is meant by it ?   65

        What does it look like   67

    How is it Done ?   71

        With a well-trained horse   71

        With a green horse   72

        With a ruined horse   74

        *How is the ruined horse taught to accept driving
            influences ?*   .   .   .   ·   .   .   76

CONTENTS

IV

EXERCISES FOR THE
FURTHER TRAINING OF RIDER AND HORSE

V

TACKLE

ILLUSTRATIONS

PLATES AT END

I

THE TRAINING OF THE RIDER

IT IS VERY SELDOM INDEED that the young rider can predict at the outset of his training in which way he will later on practise the sport. All he knows is that he wants to learn to ride a horse. The road, however, that everyone has to follow in the beginning, is the same one, regardless of all future purposes. On a suitable, quiet horse any normal person should be able to move about fairly decently at the three gaits after thirty lessons. One man—who will perhaps ride once a week for reasons of health —will be satisfied with this result; another will take his sport more seriously, and a third may even make it a profession. To the first the horse is nothing but a means of transport; to the others, riding may mean an end in itself, perhaps even an art. The simpler the task the easier it is to reach the goal; the higher ambition and sporting spirit pitch the aims, the more hard work and industrious zeal will perforce be required. No one can become a real master in the saddle who has not for years and years seriously endeavoured to gain a new experience every day; and even he will have to say: 'I live and learn'.

The training of the rider comprises three things: 'SEAT', 'FEELING', and 'INFLUENCE'. Of these, it cannot be said that one is more important than the other, because the three are absolutely inseparable and depend on each other. Likewise, it is not possible first to acquire a good seat[1] and later on, independently, to learn all the rest.

During the very first lesson one not only begins with learning

---

[1] If it is said of a rider that 'he has a good seat' this remark, which apparently refers to his 'seat' only, must also include his 'feel' and his 'influence'.

how to 'sit', but also how to 'feel' and how to 'influence'. We often hear that 'the seat' is the basis of all riding. To some extent that is certainly so. But it must never be forgotten that the rider's position is in every smallest detail determined by the influence he wants to exert on the horse. And here again, both 'seat' and 'influence' are determined by the 'feel'.

It is therefore imperative that, from the very beginning, the rider should learn how to 'feel'. He must learn to feel whether he sits his horse comfortably and loosely, and whether he keeps in the saddle by balance alone; he must learn to feel whether he is really in harmony with the horse's movements, and how to act with his back- and loin-muscles, his weight, his thighs, and the reins. Unless he has acquired a 'feel' for all this, it is impossible for the rider to sit his horse really well, i.e. in a relaxed and supple way. He will only cling on to the animal in whatever position was taught him or which he has somehow or other acquired, and this, of course, has nothing to do with 'riding'. Such a 'seat' would be wrong, quite wrong, however 'good looking' or 'correct' it may appear to some people. It cannot be good, because it is rigid and without 'feel'.

Of all the many riders who believe that they 'know all about it' there are in fact very few who really come up to the mark; most of them over-rate their capacity and under-rate the task. When difficulties arise they do not blame themselves but the horse—or, if they want to appear really clever, attribute their difficulties to the animal's 'faulty conformation' which, even if it did exist, would seldom have any appreciable influence. This is the reason why so many horses are badly trained and especially those of whom it is said that they are 'well made'. Well-made horses are rare, quite as rare as really good riders.

Since every rider will sooner or later come across one difficulty or another, it is important that, as part of his training, he occupy himself—at least in theory—with the possible reasons for a horse's misbehaviour and how to deal with them.

Everyone who wants justly to call himself—or herself—a

'rider' should ponder the following statement very seriously: 99 per cent of all horses have quite a number of bad habits which are commonly put down to 'disobedience'. And 99 per cent of all riders do not understand how to break their horses of such habits. They do not even try to understand the methods by which such habits can be got rid of. They may, of course, have heard that a horse must be 'collected' or 'put to the aids', but they are satisfied with having heard it. And so, inevitably, although unintentionally, they get their own horses into all kinds of bad habits. They do not think it worth their while to consider whether it is really so difficult to 'collect' the horse (see p. 65) as is often said; and consequently, they never find out that it is ever so much easier than they think—or, at least just as easy, as to learn how to 'follow the horse's movements' (see p. 12). There again, 99 per cent of all riders do not know how to 'follow' the horse's movements and how to 'stick to the saddle', because they did not learn how to 'brace the back' (see p. 15). The thing which every child can do on a swing is too difficult for most riders to try in the saddle ! All this should make every rider think whether he cannot perhaps, for his own good, get behind all this 'black magic' !

HOW DOES THE RIDER LEARN TO SIT?

The meaning of the expression 'seat' is often misinterpreted. It refers less to 'the position of the limbs'—as is commonly assumed—than to whether the rider:

(1) sits his horse 'loosely',
(2) keeps in the saddle by 'balance', and
(3) has learnt to 'follow the horse's movements'.

If a rider masters these three elements of the 'seat', he sits well and pleasantly, masters his limbs and can keep them in such a position as his 'feel' tells him and as the necessary 'aids' or 'influences' require.

The conception of a so-called 'correct seat' is the source of a dangerous over-estimation of the value of external appearance, and has done a lot of damage. (Fig. 1, Fig. 2.)

There are many ways in which to sit on a horse and one can learn a lot by watching other riders, but, just as any picture[1] of

---

In order to emphasize the danger which lies in the over-valuation of a 'prototype' no picture is shown of the 'correct seat.'

BALANCE,

LOOSENESS and

FOLLOWING THE MOVEMENT
OF THE HORSE

can hardly be shown graphically, nor can 'feel' be depicted. By omitting a picture, however, the importance of a good seat is not belittled, but particular attention is drawn to those elements which really matter.

Fig. 1

a 'correct seat', or its description, automatically induces the beginner to imitate this stereotyped form, it is likewise wrong for an instructor to make his pupil sit down somehow 'correctly'. This must needs lead to stiffness, which is the worst fault of all. (See also p. 10.)

The problem 'How does the rider learn to sit?' is one of utmost importance. It cannot easily be explained, nor in few words. The two questions frequently asked by beginners: 'Do I sit all right?' or 'What do I still do wrong?' are answered

[1] Fig. 3 : The 'correct' seat.

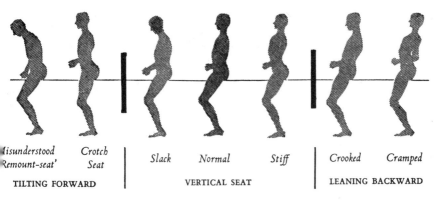

Misunderstood 'Remount-seat'	Crotch Seat	Slack	Normal	Stiff	Crooked	Cramped
TILTING FORWARD			VERTICAL SEAT		LEANING BACKWARD	

Fig. 2. VARIOUS TYPES OF SEAT

simultaneously with it. By rights, every rider should be able to answer these last two questions for himself. For he alone can tell if he really sits 'comfortably' and if he has learnt to 'feel'—provided always that he already understands the things that matter and that he has grasped the meaning of the three principles: 'Balance', 'Looseness', and 'Following the horse's movements'.

The position of the limbs which then results, with ease and quite automatically, is determined by the influences which are to be exerted. 'Legs' and 'hands' will therefore not be discussed in answering the question, 'How does the rider learn to sit?' but will be treated in connexion with 'influences' or 'aids' by legs and hands (see p. 26), and the 'position of the body' will be dealt with in connexion with 'influences by the weight'. (See p. 33.)

BALANCE

The very first thing the rider must acquire is 'balance'. By balance alone he must keep in the saddle and not by means of his arms and legs. The body should rest vertically upon the two pelvic bones and the crotch, i.e. on three points of support, exactly at the lowest point of the saddle. It is important that this lowest point should be right in the middle of the saddle, not towards the pommel or towards the cantle as, unfortunately, is more often than not the case with badly built or poorly fitted saddles. The correct position of the saddle is shown on the horse in Fig. 24. Arms and legs have nothing to do with balance and can only be of help to the rider if he has lost his balance and has to 'hang on in desperation'.

The quickest way for the young rider to find his balance is to begin with stirrups at a slow walk and then at a quiet trot. The horse must be quiet and is best bridled with side reins. The less the beginner is shouted at the more he can concentrate upon his balance. If the horse has side reins his movements are more comfortable and the rider will be less tossed about. It is very important to put the beginner on a quiet, well-mannered horse with soft and agreeable movements. Stirrups are necessary at this stage because they make the beginner feel a little safer, and enable him the sooner to gain confidence and loosen up, for there will be so little reason for 'cramping'. Should the beginner have difficulties the reason will probably be found in the horse having 'too much movement'. If this is the case the mount must be changed, because the easier the beginner finds things the quicker he will acquire confidence, and the sooner he will find his balance.

As soon as 'balance' is maintained fairly persistently (and this should be the case after a few lessons), it ought to be tested by doing away with the stirrups. This, however, should be done gradually so as not to destroy the newly established confidence. If the confidence is lost the rider will again become muscle-bound and cling on to the horse by mere force. Falls ought to be carefully avoided because they often destroy confidence altogether and consequently lead to stiffness and rigidity, especially with riders who have not much nerve. Riding without stirrups should be practised step by step; the rider ought to grope his way to it, as it were, trying at first a few strides and, if he feels safe enough, gradually increasing the periods, at the same time trying to turn his head and to do physical exercises. All this will strengthen the confidence in his balance.

Balance is a sort of gymnastics which every rider soon grasps. It must be fortified by learning how to put the back muscles into positive action (see p. 15). Only then will the rider be able to find the proper place in the saddle. Without proper explanation of what is meant by 'action of the back-muscles' and 'following the horse's movement' there is a grave danger of commands like, 'sit up straight', 'lean forward' or 'lean backward', leading to rigidity and to a 'hollow back'. And this must be avoided in all circumstances. If the rider hollows his back he forces his buttocks out of the saddle and, thus giving up the firm basis of his seat, loses all possibility of balancing himself.

The pupil must learn to rely quite automatically on his balance, as, for instance, when riding a bicycle, when it is a *conditio sine qua non*. Only perfect balance will enable the rider to acquire a subtle 'feel' for every movement of his horse and for the influence of his weight. A rider who is not perfectly balanced will never be 'moulded into one' with his horse.

Balance can be said to be perfect if the rider feels safe enough without stirrups in turns, bends and corners or in serpentines without having to 'hang on', and if he can nonchalantly turn round in the saddle, move, and talk. This the rider can judge best for himself.

Even the more advanced rider should test himself repeatedly by riding without stirrups, and, if he does not *feel at home*, should confess to himself that the reason can only be a certain stiffness which prevents him from keeping his proper balance. Otherwise he *would* 'feel at home'.

LOOSENESS, SUPPLENESS

'Looseness' means the condition in which all the rider's joints are loose and slack and the muscles relaxed and not

involuntarily tense. This, however, does not mean that the
limbs should flop about. The rider must consciously control
his muscles all the time, just as the acrobat does when executing
an elegant and easy-looking swing on the horizontal bar. The
difficulty is that the rider does not always realize whether he
tightens a muscle or not. It is certain, however, that there
must be a stiffness somewhere if the rider does not sit comfortably, if he can assume a certain position only by force and if he
cramps himself on to the horse. As soon as he has got the
proper feeling for balance and has banished all fear, the cause
for stiffness is eliminated. The way is paved to 'looseness'.

We often hear that physical exercises on horseback strengthen
the rider's confidence and improve 'looseness' and 'balance'.[1]
Certainly turning round in the saddle, moving, talking,
whistling, smoking, and doing a few 'jerks' will increase his
confidence and help him to 'relax'; but this only holds good if
he has already acquired a fair balance and with it a certain
amount of confidence. However, as is often the case with
slogans upon which a system is built without investigation of
their justification, much too much time and labour is usually
spent on these physical exercises. If they are carried too far
the rider may lose his balance. Not infrequently young riders
are to be seen who, after acquiring a fair amount of relaxation,
relapse again into 'hanging on' with their thighs and legs as a
result of the overdoing of these exercises.

Riding across country helps towards looseness at least as
much as physical jerks, and it affords the additional advantage of
making the rider better acquainted with his horse and its
behaviour. A foreign language can be learnt in its own
country better than from books and grammars. When one
has first learnt to understand the language it is easy later on to
learn the grammar.

---

[1] 'Balance' and 'Looseness' are closely related to each other, although
they are not identical. The rider must loosen up before he can balance.
But it does not follow that he can balance after he has loosened up.

Unlike 'physical jerks on horseback', the importance of which, as has been said, is frequently over-estimated, 'physical jerks on foot' are generally neglected. Yet it is quite clear that a faulty carriage of the rider, which may have its cause in physical defects or in a lack of physical training, must needs influence his seat on horseback. But there is a difference between a faulty bearing—which only influences, so to say, 'the picture'—and those faults which influence the actual riding. We must also distinguish between innate physical defects, i.e. actual malformations of the body, and bad habits which a person may have acquired and which may show only on foot or perhaps in the saddle too. All such shortcomings should be discussed between riding master and pupil, preferably between lessons. When the faulty carriage is brought about by fear, lack of confidence, or too lively a horse, instructor and pupil can discuss the necessary remedies together. But where the physical defects or bad habits of the rider are concerned, the riding master only can help, by giving advice which ought to be strictly followed by the pupil.

Therefore all 'physical jerks on foot' which are meant to eradicate bad habits should—as opposed to 'physical jerks on horseback'—never be executed collectively by a whole riding class, but always individually, because these bad habits are unlikely to be the same with all riders.

The first and most commonly met with difficulties are pains in the thighs, caused by the unaccustomed stretching of the thigh muscles. People who suffer badly from such pains will later on have more or less continuous trouble with their legs. One can only 'sit well' and 'loosely' if one sits comfortably. If sitting in the saddle causes discomfort; if the rider has difficulty in keeping the legs close to the horse, just behind the girth; or if the legs do not, so to say, hang there quite naturally, then the rider is somehow too narrow in the breech. This is the case with two out of three persons when they first begin to ride, and rather too little attention is paid to it. Even if the

pains disappear after a few days, as would be natural, the rider
still struggles, finding it difficult to keep his legs in the right
place, and does not realize the cause of his struggles. No will-
power, no brave efforts, no pluck will prevent the muscles
from getting stale if they have continually to be forced into a
certain position.

Exercises like 'stretching the legs sideways' and 'straddling
the legs on foot' help to stretch the inner
muscles of the thighs, but if they are to be
effective these exercises must be repeated
morning, noon, and night. There is
hardly another, and certainly no better
way, of influencing and improving the
position of the upper leg than by such
'physical jerks on foot'.

It is advisable to ride a narrow horse
until such time as these exercises have had
the desired result.

Other faults, such as stiffness of the
ankles or the loins, a rounded back,
unequal hips, or the like, should be
remedied in similar ways. Stiffness in the
wrists is also detrimental, just as it is when
playing the piano or the violin.

All these deficiencies, however, cannot
be cured in those short hours during
which the rider is actually in the saddle—
and that is the worst of it. If, therefore,
the pupil does not strictly follow the
instructor's advice he must not be surprised
that these deficiencies badly affect the com-

Fig. 3.

THE GRENADIER'S
SEAT

*(The wooden puppet. The
result of profuse 'seat
corrections')*

fort and the looseness of his seat and that his difficulties with
'feel' and 'influence' continue. For this reason it was pointed
out a little while ago that frequently these 'physical jerks on
foot' are not valued sufficiently.

The so-called 'seat corrections' constitute one of the gravest dangers to 'looseness of seat'. This may sound paradoxical to many who will probably ask: 'But mustn't you tell a man how to sit and shouldn't you correct his seat?' Yet it is not as paradoxical as it appears. 'Seat corrections', old favourites with many instructors, in the end serve no useful purpose. They squeeze the rider into a 'prescribed form' and are definitely a seducement to stiffness and rigidity.

Position and carriage of body and limbs depend on their use and on their influences, i.e. on the way in which they are to act upon the horse. This position can therefore only be improved in connexion with the aids and with the gradual acquiring of the necessary feel. All this, however, must not be understood to mean that the improving of the seat should be neglected! On the contrary—it should impress upon the reader the fact that only a riding instruction in its entirety can produce a 'good seat', i.e. if the rider also learns 'to feel' and to 'influence'.

As an example, each 'half-halt' (see p. 115) enables the rider to observe whether the horse obeys the aids; it animates his 'feel', and induces him to straighten his body, to make himself, so to speak, longer, and to let his legs act upon the horse's sides: in other words, it 'improves his seat'. Naturally, the rider can only feel whether the half-halt was effective or not if he is thoroughly loosened up. On the other hand, commands for 'seat corrections', such as 'sit up straight' or 'sit erect' or 'bring your chest forward', may make the rider stiff because he will concentrate upon 'sitting erect' or 'sitting straight'. But a rider should not learn to 'sit straight' but to *ride*.

If pupil and master pay adequate attention to these 'half-halts', whose value for developing seat, feel and influence is inestimable, all 'seat corrections' will soon be superfluous. It should be realized that the first 'attention!' preceding every word of command, should always be answered by the rider with a 'half-halt', and this dispenses with all such commands as: 'sit up straight', 'chest forward', 'make yourself longer', and so on. If in a class the execution of these 'half-halts' is carefully watched, all the pupils will automatically correct their seats, thereby improving their feel and their influences.

For the riding master it is all the same whether he watches the execution of his 'attention!', preceding a command, or whether he supervises the execution of his 'seat corrections'. For the rider, however, it is not all the same. He should never 'just' straighten up, or 'just' bring his chest forward, or 'just' sit erect. He should always give himself—and the horse—a 'half-halt'. That means much more. 'Straightening up' must be done to a particular purpose and must never be stiff. For a 'half-halt' the rider must combine the 'making himself longer', 'straightening up' and 'closing his legs', with 'sticking to the saddle', 'feel' and 'following the horse's movements'. Only a rider who can correctly execute a 'half-halt' will acquire a fine, supple and good seat.

HOW DOES THE RIDER LEARN TO 'FOLLOW THE HORSE'S MOVE-MENT', AND TO STICK TO THE SADDLE?

All difficulties begin with the command 'trot on', i.e. when the rider begins to be 'tossed' or 'bumped'. Some horses 'toss' more, others less. The softer or lower the movements of the horse the easier the rider will get along. But if the rider is later on requested to go at a 'better pace' and the side reins are left off, or if he changes on to another horse with 'more move-ment', he will still find this bumping rather uncomfortable.

The inexperienced beginner first of all tries to fight against this bumping by clinging on to the horse with legs and thighs. This will hardly produce the desired result! Moreover, the discomfort will be followed by soreness and stiffness.

The cause of this difficulty, namely, 'being left behind', will be discussed in the chapter dealing with the 'influence of the weight' (see p. 33). The remedy for it is proper action of the back-muscles. Very few people have a proper conception of the play of the muscles in the back, which in everyday life are never tightened consciously. The following chapter will deal thoroughly with the activity of these muscles, because it is of particular importance and needs thorough explanation. Unfortunately, although a person may have grasped the idea of 'bracing the back-muscles', it does not yet follow that proper use can be made of them on horseback.

By 'bracing the back', as we shall call it henceforth, it is easy to move a swing, and in the same way we can make a horse go forward. And, once the horse is moving, we can similarly avoid being 'left behind'. This is what is meant by 'following the horse's movement', or 'being in harmony with the horse', or more shortly 'follow the horse'. As soon as one has learnt properly to 'move on', one should also be able to 'follow'; if one does not master the first it is a dead certainty that one will never do either in the proper manner.

There are many riders with a good many years of practice who have never thoroughly grasped this principal basis of a good seat, this elementary foundation of all refined aids! One cannot possibly rely upon chance or time, telling oneself: 'Oh! that'll come in time all right!' It will not! *It has to be tried and it must be learnt.* For this purpose a well-trained horse is the best teacher because it reacts immediately and noticeably upon this 'back-muscle' action.

If the rider in 'moving on' not only uses his legs, but also brings his back and loins into play, he will find that he obtains the desired result with a minimum of leg pressure. The more use the rider makes of his back the less leg pressure will he require.

If the rider tries this back-muscle action for the 'parade',[1] he will notice that its execution feels entirely different from what he has been used to. Previously, without the aid of his back, he stopped his horse at the head by pressure on the bit, which sometimes had to be quite considerable. If the back comes

[1] 'Parade' is the school rider's expression for 'Halt'. THE TRANSLATOR.

into action the whole horse is shoved together and pushed forward. He runs up to the bit and there, if the reins don't give, finds sufficient resistance to stop him. It requires a minimum of pressure on the bit to make the horse understand that instead of going forward at a better pace, he should stop. At such a 'parade' the rider will feel that the horse is lower at the croup than in front. (See Fig. 29 and Plate 4.)

The best way to develop a good feel for the effect of 'bracing the back' are frequent repetitions of moving on and halting—walking on, trotting on and halting—in other words, continuous changes of gait, from halt to walk, from walk to trot, from trot to halt, and so on. If this feel cannot be acquired on one horse, one must change over to another, until finally one *has* felt it. A rider who doesn't do that will never acquire the feel for this all-important action !

It is imperative to get a decided feel of the difference between moving on and halting by 'bracing the back' and moving on and halting without this action. Once a rider has acquired this feel to a certain degree he can, by continuous practice, prevent himself from being bumped at the trot.

At a quiet trot this back-muscle action pushes the rider's buttocks and his centre of gravity forward and the lower end of his spine rests firmly in the saddle. The rider—if one may say so—sucks himself on to the saddle by means of his loins and thighs. This makes for a very close contact between rider and horse without necessitating any tiresome muscular exertions. The feel for this is best acquired on well-trained horses who have not too much movement. Frequent changes of gait—i.e. moving on, trotting, halting, moving on again, etc.—will be found of great help, for the action of bracing the back is carried over from the halt and the walk into the trot. By bracing the back more or less firmly one can sit tighter or looser in the saddle. The higher the horse's movement and the faster the trot the more must the rider bring his back into action. And it must be repeated that it is absolutely imperative to try this out on different horses as soon as one thinks one has mastered the secret !

The stage of a perfect 'sticking to the saddle' is reached when the rider can sit a good middle trot on various horses. He must not bump in the saddle but constantly 'follow' it, i.e. sit so tight and quiet as to make it possible to keep a piece of paper under his seat by mere action of his weight.

'Following the horse's movements' is always a matter of suppleness and sensitive feeling. It cannot be hard or rigid and should never be associated with muscular exertion or noticeable movements. Even the most highly-trained and scrupulous observer can therefore not recognize it other than by its effect. A rider who properly 'follows the horse' looks much better and is certainly 'bumped' less than others. A hollow back, jerky, or swaying movements of the backbone are not the same thing as this all-important 'bracing of the back'. It is possible that a rider in doing it may once in a while appear to be leaning backwards, but, just by leaning backwards, one cannot learn to 'follow the horse'. (See Plate 4.)

Often the advice is given to a rider to 'let his back swing with the horse'. That is all very well, but no help for a tiro. This 'swinging with the horse' does not result from a passive 'letting the back swing'. It is a positive muscle action, a conscious pushing forward. In exactly the same way on a swing we can, by bracing the back, increase its oscillations, whereas a passive 'swinging with it' will most certainly bring it to a stop.

'BACK-MUSCLE ACTION'

'Bracing the back', as the phrase is to be understood for the rider's purposes, is important for all influences and aids, so important indeed, that it is hardly possible to give correct aids unless one properly masters this action.

The feel for it can only be acquired by trying it out. Only the horse and his own feel can tell the rider whether it has

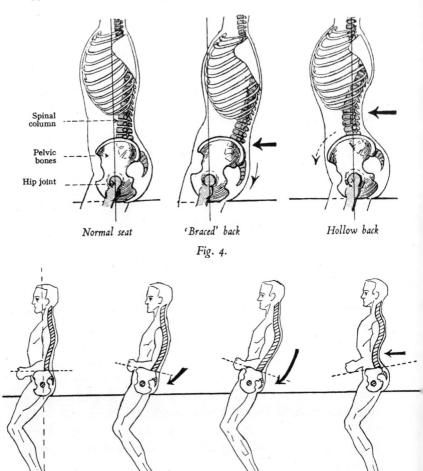

Spinal
column

Pelvic
bones

Hip joint

Normal seat   'Braced' back   Hollow back

Fig. 4.

Normal   Braced   Back braced   Hollow
seat   back   a bit more   back

Fig. 5.

been tried out sufficiently. And as long as the rider does
not notice the effect it has upon his horse, he has not
acquired the feel for it. A 'feeling', however, excludes

rigidity and even bracing the back must never result in stiffness.

The muscles to be tightened are not the 'spinal muscles', as the anatomist would call them; but in the end it does not matter what muscles they are, as long as the rider has the right conception of the movement.

At a normal position the backbone, or spine, has a curved shape. When 'bracing the back' the lower end of the spine and the rump-bone (os sacrum), which connects the spinal column with the pelvic bones, are pushed forward. The pelvis is thereby pivoted, being raised at the front and

Fig. 6 A.

lowered at the rear, thus preventing the body from tilting forward. The gravest mistake is a 'hollow back', which has just the opposite effect, namely tilting the pelvis towards the front.

In practising the pupil can talk, whistle, and smoke, all of which will be useful in preventing rigidity. The movement proper is best studied by the following exercises:

Bilateral Tightening of the Muscles:

    (1) On a swing the back is braced for the forward swing and slackened for the backward swing. (Fig. 6A.)

2

(2) If you lie down on the floor you can only raise your buttocks by bracing the back. (Fig. 6B.)

Fig. 6 B.

(3) Standing in front of a table with a book protruding over its edge you can push the book on to the table without resorting to the hands, just by bracing the back. (Fig. 6C, Fig. 6D.)

This last comparison is a striking example of the difference between a 'braced back' and a 'hollow back'. Bracing the

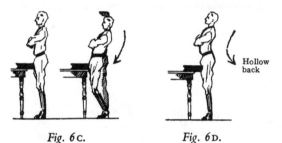

Hollow back

Fig. 6 C.   Fig. 6 D.

back pushes the buttocks forward, which is the main point in riding—whereas a hollow back thrusts them out to the rear. 'Bringing the chest forward' and 'closing in the shoulder blades' are mostly the result of a hollow back.

(4) If you sit on a chair leaning against its back you can slide your thighs and buttocks forward by bracing your back. (Fig. 6E.)

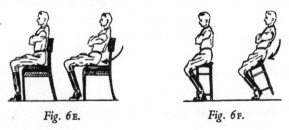

Fig. 6E.   Fig. 6F.

(5) If you straddle a light stool or paper-basket, or similar object, you can easily tilt it by bracing the back. It is, of course, essential that the legs should not rest on the floor in front of the line of gravity but to the right and left of it. In this way you can even tilt a heavy chair, if you sit far enough forward. (Fig. 6f.)

Do not be satisfied with reading these explanations and looking at the pictures, for although they will help you to understand the movement, you will not have yet *felt* it. You must *try it out*. Even if you have a definite feel for this 'bracing the back', it still needs special practice on horseback to enable you to use it to the best advantage in riding! (See also Plate 4.)

Unilateral Tightening of the Back-Muscles (pushing forward one hip or one pelvic bone):

Practising unilateral actions of the loins is just as important as the foregoing exercises. All 'collected riding', each bend, each corner, and the seat at the canter, depend on the rider's ability to push the inner hip[1] and pelvic bone forward. This must also be tried out until the feel for it is acquired with certainty.

(1) A swing can be brought into a *swaying* motion by unilateral forward pressure.

(2) If you lie on the floor again you can raise the right or left buttock by tightening the respective side of the back-muscles.

(3) The book protruding over the table edge can be pushed forward *and sideways* by tightening only one side of the loin-muscles.

Bracing the back is just as easy or just as difficult to understand and to learn in the first few lessons as later on. The

[1] The expressions, 'inner hip', 'inner leg', 'inner hand', etc., will henceforth be used to denote the 'hand' on which we are riding, e.g. in going on the 'right hand' (circle on the right hand), the right hip will be the 'inner hip', the right leg the 'inner leg', and so forth. THE TRANSLATOR.

loin- or back-muscles can be tightened in various degrees like all other muscles and 'aids' can therefore be given with more or less action of the loins. It is possible to brace or tighten the back-muscles very strongly and thereby to push the buttocks forward, but it is also possible to brace the back just sufficiently to prevent one from sliding backward in the saddle. All this must be tried out so that it can be put into actual practice instead of remaining an empty phrase. (See Plate 4.)

Never forget that bracing the back is the basis of adjusting the seat, of walking and trotting on and of executing a parade ! Without back-muscle action effective aids are impossible and each halt will just be a pull at the reins. Without the back-muscle action, a 'good seat' is impossible, and lack of this elementary basis is the primary cause of all bad habits in a horse.

The most common mistakes which are made in connexion with this back-muscle action are :

(1) Most riders believe that it is not necessary to try out these movements on foot, but that it suffices to have grasped the idea. The result is that, when they get into the saddle, they lack the proper feel and do not know which muscles to put into action.

(2) Most riders do not sufficiently practise this action as a proper exercise on horseback. The feel for it can only be acquired by continuous concentration when walking on, trotting on, or making a 'parade'. At the same time, of course, the thighs ought never to be forgotten and should always have close contact with the horse. If this feel does not come on one horse, the only course is to change horses until finally one has felt it.

We often hear that a rider has 'a lot of backbone' or that he has 'no back'. These expressions are misleading. All riders have more or less the same amount of 'back', but they do not

all know equally well how to operate with it. Most people
have sufficient muscular
strength, so that there can
be little danger of over-
exertion by undue use of these
muscles. Real 'back aches'
are something entirely
different. They can be caused
by the rider getting too much
bumping, or by too long a
lesson. Such pains, however,
can hardly be put down to
too strong an action of the
back-muscles !

HOW DOES THE RIDER LEARN TO 'FEEL'?

The 'feel' of a rider, or
what can perhaps best be
expressed by the phrase 'true
horsemanship', consists of the
ability properly to judge one's
own seat, influences, and aids,
as well as an appreciation of
the 'giving' of the horse, the
swing of his movements and
his attention and concentration. A rider must be able to
say or to 'feel how his horse is
going', what influences or
aids are necessary and how
strongly they ought to be
applied. He also ought to
know or 'feel' whether a single

Fig. 7. BRACING THE BACK ON
HORSEBACK

(see also Fig. 29 and Plate 4)

application was enough or whether they are to be repeated and if the purpose has been attained. 'Feel' is something that the rider must acquire all by himself; others can only help to awaken it. They can promote it by correct explanation and by teaching him self-examination; they can promote it by the correct selection of lessons and by the manner in which their execution is demanded and supervised by the instructor. It doesn't matter *that* lessons are being executed, but it matters *how* they are executed !

In the following paragraphs self-examination will be thoroughly discussed in connexion with all aids and influences, because it is only by such self-examination, i.e. by intelligent *thinking*, that 'feel' can be created, promoted and shaped. It is of advantage for the development of 'feel' if the rider starts with easy lessons and does not proceed to the more difficult ones until he has learnt to execute correctly the easy ones, and until he has learnt to judge for himself whether a certain lesson has been properly executed or not.

If a rider is unable to cope with a difficult task he should not be satisfied with a poor or imperfect result, for this completely kills 'feel'; in such a case he should ask his instructor. An instructor will never resent this, whereas he would certainly take it as a sign of indifference and lack of ambition if the pupil attempted to deceive him, and he would be inclined to take less pains with that pupil in future. But a pupil who shows keen interest is always an incentive to the instructor, whose interest in turn becomes greater. An example will make this clear:

For the execution of a 'halt' (see p. 115), the instructor orders the rider to act simultaneously with his back, his legs and the reins. The rider, however, feels that if he increases the leg-pressure his horse will not pull up, but go forward. Consequently, he omits leg-pressure and merely pulls at the reins. Most riders have had this experience and have noticed the contradiction, but they do not bother to talk about it. This is a mistake ! The beginner should talk about these things to his instructor and he should then try the 'halt' on other, possibly better horses, until he has really learned its correct execution.

Horses used for instructional purposes very soon get stale, however well schooled or 'made' they may be, and very often they get blamed for mistakes. But the real cause is that the continual change of riders (as is inevitable in riding schools), must needs make them numb. It is very difficult to keep them up to the mark and therefore not always possible for a rider to acquire the 'feel' for some things on such horses. Yet even stale horses will readily accept the right aids if their application has been learnt on well-made, sensitive horses. For the promotion of a good feel, frequent change of horses is absolutely essential, because every horse gives a different 'feel'. Change forces the rider to adapt the emphasis of his aids to the sensitiveness of each new horse, and consequently a new 'feel' is acquired.

The best instructor, and the one who alone is able to impart the proper feel to the rider, is the horse. He never tires and is ever patient in telling his rider where and when he has made a mistake. It is only necessary to know the horse's language and to pay attention to his corrections. Naturally, beginners very often fail to understand this language and they think a lot of themselves when they blame the 'bally beast' for being stale and feel-less, old, or 'badly made'.

The warnings which a horse can give are of various types. Some of them refer to bad habits of the riders, others to lack of attention. Most of them, however, are provoked by complete lack of harmony in the rider's influences. If a horse throws his head up and down it is as if he were sighing: 'Don't jerk at my mouth !' If a horse tries to kick at the rider's leg he is saying: 'Don't tickle me with your spur !' Or if a horse continually twists his tail he is saying: 'Your legs are too fidgety and you tickle me !' And if a horse leans heavily on the bit he means: 'Your hands are too hard'. Naturally, for the horse is always just as hard as the hand of the rider. Pressure produces counter-pressure, as in life. And if a rider complains of the hardness of his horse's mouth he is, in most cases, complaining of his own clumsy hands. Many horses gradually get harder and more feel-less in their mouths if they are constantly being pulled about; but if even the hardest mouthed of such horses are treated sensitively and quietly, their mouths will get softer in no time.

When talking of 'feel' most riders think first of all of their hands, and yet it is most important that a rider learn to feel not through his hands but through his seat. The first manifestation arises for the beginner in the very first few lessons, when his horse, at the halt, rests one hind leg or sets it back. This occurs very often after a full 'halt' (see below). Even the worst

Fig. 8. FIRST OPPOR-
TUNITY TO ACQUIRE
'FEEL'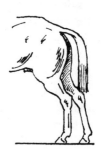

beginner will quite unconsciously feel that all of a sudden he is much lower on one side than on the other. He does not know why. Often enough we notice that he tries to level himself by shifting about in the saddle, straightening up his body, standing in the stirrups, sitting down again and so on, until he finally gives up and resigns himself to the inevitable. He does not pay any further attention to the fact that his shifting about in the saddle has not had the desired result. Had he, however, by gentle leg-pressure, urged the horse to make a step forward, so as to stand straight on his four legs, he would have felt himself restored to the straight position, the lower side of the horse to have got higher again. The little sketch above will remind the reader to look out for such details.

It is important to note from this example that every rider can really feel a lot more than he thinks he can. If such a feel (as, in this case of the horse resting on one foot) does not come home to him, it means that he does not pay any attention to it. Had he been able to *explain* the incident he would also have been aware of his *feel*. A sensation does not become a feel until we are conscious of it—*cogito ergo sum!*

Thus, every rider can best judge for himself if he has learned to 'follow the horse', because possibly he alone knows if he is bumping about in the saddle, and he alone can tell whether he can avoid this bumping. If his feel is not yet developed to such an extent that he can keep a piece of paper under his buttocks, then no compliments on his alleged 'good seat' or 'good legs' should convince him of his efficiency, and he should γνῶθι σεαυτόν confess to himself that he has not yet grasped the most important principles of the 'seat'.

There are quite a number of riders, including many who have been riding for a long time, who, put upon their honour, would have to admit that they cannot tell on which leg their horse is leading at the canter. A rider who cannot *feel* when his horse is cantering on the wrong leg, cannot have a good seat. It is impossible to tell a rider more clearly that his seat is wrong ! (See p. 132.)

In general a rider can best convince himself of how much he has learned by putting his knowledge to the test on a very sensitive horse. He can check on a horse :

(*a*) with a soft back . . . . whether he has learned to follow, supply the movements of the horse ;

(*b*) with a sensitive mouth . . . . whether his hands are 'light' ;

(*c*) on a ticklish horse . . . . whether his legs are steady and quiet.

The more sensitive the horse the clearer will be his message to the rider. Feel can only be acquired by practice, and in turn it helps us along in practice, but only if we let ourselves be helped. Without a lot of trying and self-criticism and without the proper persevering will and energy, no man can ever learn a thing, no matter how great his experience and extended his practice.

HOW DOES THE RIDER LEARN TO 'INFLUENCE'?

The rider can influence the horse with his legs, his back, his weight and the reins. Each of these influences acts according to its nature:

the legs, in a driving,
the reins, in a restraining,
the weight, in a bending way,
while the back-muscle action is the necessary link, connecting these various influences.

In the following paragraphs they will be discussed one by one.

The emphasis with which these 'influences' are to be exerted is always determined by the sensitiveness of the horse. Not one of them, however, can be exerted with such force as to constitute a physical compulsion for the horse. There is the possibility of innumerable variations of degree and shade in these influences, according to how each is exerted in combination with the others. The *combinations* of these influences by which the rider conveys his wishes to the horse, are called '*aids*'. There are 'aids' for walking on, trotting on, cantering on, for turns, 'halts', half-halts, and so on (see Lessons, pp. 113 and following). Each of these 'aids' consists of several 'influences' which must be exerted simultaneously if the horse is to understand what the rider wants. We therefore do not talk of leg-'aids' or rein-'aids', but always of 'influences' of the leg or 'influences' of the reins and so on.

It might seem logical that the rider should first try out the 'influences' separately in order that, when familiar with them, he could give the proper 'aids'. Unfortunately, this cannot possibly be done on horseback, because the horse can only respond to influences if several of them are exerted *in combination*; otherwise they are not intelligible. For instance, if we wanted to try out the effect of 'tightening the reins' without simultaneously adding the necessary back- and leg-influence, the horse will not know what to do. He can raise his head or lower it, he can make his mouth give to the pressure of the bit or he can press against it, he can throw his head about, and, in fact, can do almost anything bar one thing: understand what we want !.

The rider must therefore learn from the very beginning to give the proper 'aids'. He should start with simple aids, such as 'walk on', 'trot on' and 'halt'. These aids are the easiest because the required influences are equal on both sides of the horse (off and near) and do not require shifting of the weight.

The aids which require different leg- and rein-influences on the near side and the off side are much more difficult. It is advisable to practise the latter at the halt, because as long as the rider has to struggle for his balance while the horse is in motion, and as long as he has not yet learned completely to harmonize with the movements of the horse, he easily tends to .make himself stiff and rigid if such unilateral influences are required of him. A quiet school horse will turn at the corners without any aids at all, even if bridled with side reins, and thus teach the rider to shift his weight towards the inside; but he will not teach him the way in which the 'aids' for turning are to be given.

. Pivoting on the forehand (see p. 124) and pivoting on the haunches (see p. 126) are indispensable exercises. When tried out step by step they teach the rider how to apply the aids for turning by the different influences, right and left. When the rider has acquired the feel for the proper co-operation of his right and left influences, so that he can correctly execute the first steps of the pivot on the forelegs and on the haunches during the halt, he will have little difficulty in exerting the same in the identical combination while the horse is in motion. This affords sufficient preparation for learning the aids for riding 'in position', for turning and for cantering on, so that these aids can be given with the right feel and with the proper determination. There will be no more cause for the rider to make himself stiff. The more subtle and invisible these aids, the more perfect the harmony between rider and horse.

INFLUENCES OF THE LEGS

The lower legs act:

(a) close behind the girth, 'urging on'.

The rider acquires the feel for this in the very first few lessons when he finds that the horse, at a standstill, will go forward if both legs are pressed against him, or if they repeatedly tap his sides.

(b) about a hand behind the girth, 'pushing sideways', or (if they are to prevent side stepping) 'preventative', or 'limiting'.

This latter influence, too, the rider will learn to feel very soon when, at the halt, his horse moves his hind quarters one or two steps off the track away from the wall as the result of unilateral leg influence, or, conversely, when he makes the horse step back again towards the wall and into the track by the same leg influence.

The rider's lower leg influences the horse's hind leg on the same side. In time, the feel for this is increased and intensified to such a degree that all leg influences become more or less automatic reflex movements whose application does not require thinking about.

Whether the rider must press or tap with his legs, and the emphasis with which it is to be done, depend entirely on the sensitiveness of the horse.

A horse does not obey the leg influences because he must

perforce do so. A young horse has to be taught the meaning of leg-pressure by the aid of the whip. Even a schooled horse, if he gets stale, can quite well refuse to follow the influence of the leg or even throw himself against it. Therefore, it is important that the influences of the legs should always remain the same and always be given in the same manner. To this end the legs must, of course, retain a quiet and steady position.

Position of the Legs:

(*a*) The legs must never be stretched away from the horse. They would have to execute too wide a movement when being put into action and would thereby startle and frighten the horse. One ought to be able to keep a piece of paper between the calf and the horse's side.

(*b*) The legs must not be clamped to the horse's side, because they would get tired, and moreover the horse would not then react to a light pressure. Leg-pressure must naturally be increased for short moments; but the rider's legs 'keeping the horse in a vice-like grip' is an invention of Wild-West story-tellers. The less leg-pressure is required, the less will the rider get tired and the better will he be in harmony with his horse.

(*c*) The position of the legs should not offer any difficulties or discomfort and must be quite natural. In this, beginners often experience difficulties which can only be eliminated by exercises (see p. 9). Force and coercion can never result in looseness and natural suppleness but only in stiffness.

Length of leathers. An approximate measurement of the length of the leathers by means of the outstretched arm can be made before mounting. The precisely correct length can only be found in the saddle.

The leathers are too long if the toes have to be turned down in order to retain the stirrups, or if contact between the legs and the horse's body is lost.

They are too short if the contact with the horse is such a close one that the lower part of the leg cannot be moved freely. The reason is that the short leathers raise the lower leg and knee, thereby causing the body to leave the lowest point of the saddle. The rider thus loses the safe basis of his seat and involuntarily 'cramps on' with his legs (arm-chair seat).

If the leathers are of the proper length the legs will comfortably remain in contact with the horse's body, and the stirrups will automatically fall on to the rider's foot if he just raises his toes, should he by chance have lost the irons.

Position of feet in the stirrups. The stirrups belong under the *ball* of the foot, so that the ankles can move freely. It is necessary to push the feet right home in the stirrups only if a specially firm purchase is required, as for instance, in jumping or racing.

Angle between upper and lower leg. There is no set rule for the angle between upper and lower leg; the angle is determined by the length of the legs and the curvature of the horse's body. The longer the legs and the narrower the horse the acuter will be the angle; the shorter the legs and the rounder the horse's body, the more obtuse will the angle be. Every rider must therefore adjust the length of his leathers according to whether he rides a 'flat-sided' or a 'well ribbed up' horse.

Position of the knee. The knee should be placed as low as possible. This is not because of any special influence of the knee, but because the position of the knees decides more or less the position of the thighs and the buttocks. There ought to be as much contact with the horse as possible. If the knees are drawn up, the thighs are too nearly horizontal and in consequence the buttocks are pushed backwards, resulting in what is called the 'arm-chair' seat. The rider must know how to judge the position of his knees and how to push them down. While riding 'turns' or through corners and at the canter he must push his inner knee and his inner heel well down. This is merely a matter of feel. In bracing the back equally on both sides one must learn to push both the knees down (see p. 17), or to push the inner knee only down if the back is braced unilaterally (see p. 19). This movement depends on pushing forward one or both pelvic bones, whereby the same muscles come into action. If the rider has learned to accomplish this action, he will find it easy to bring his knees down at the same time.

However, lowering the knees has its limits:

(1) Contact with the horse by means of the lower legs must not be lost, as can very easily happen to tall, long-legged riders on small horses.

(2) The legs should not be placed too far backwards; they must be close to the girth if they are to urge the horse forward.

(3) The solid basis in the saddle on three points (see p. 5) must not be lost, otherwise a 'fork seat' is the result.

Knee grip. 'Knee grip' means a close pressing of the knees on to the horse's body.

The knee is a joint, controlling movement of the lower legs and therefore its freedom must not be impaired. It should never be pressed very hard against the horse's body as that would restrict its freedom. Knee grip is only required in order to provide a safe support in exceptional conditions; it is used, for example, by cavalrymen in riding an attack, by jockeys in racing, and for jumping (see p. 170).

The toes. The toes are kept pointing slightly away from the horse. Their position is regulated automatically by the movements of the legs. If the toes point exactly towards the front, parallel with the horse's body, the rider will, when bending the knee, just be able to slide his calves along the horse's body without exerting an appreciable pressure and therefore without adequate influence. If the toes point at a right angle towards the horse, the lower legs will be found to 'clamp', and the rider be unable to use them sensitively.

A rider who has to have the correct position of his thighs confirmed by others, has no feel. It is something which every one must be able to judge for himself, because only the rider himself can feel whether his legs are placed comfortably, whether the leathers are of the right length, whether he is able to hold the stirrups and whether he has a constant light contact with the horse enabling him at any time to exert a sensitive influence. Even the most expert rider must constantly test this particular feel to make sure that he is not deceiving himself —as is very often the case, especially as regards the legs ! For this reason, experienced riders will now and again resort to riding without stirrups for some time. Beginners should bear this well in mind !

We should also make sure from time to time that that light contact with the horse is really being maintained, and that we do not only imagine it. This is best done in such a way that by unilateral leg influence the horse's hind legs are made to step sideways, first half a step to the one side, then half a step to the other side. It can be done during the halt or in motion. The execution of this test is so subtle that an onlooker will not notice it at all. Yet the rider will definitely know if his feel has deceived him or not, for either he will have to carry out quite a movement with his legs (because they are too far away from the horse), or he will be able to manage (correctly) by just slightly increasing the contact. The more often this test is carried out the more will the feel for it be developed.

An apparently good leg-position which only *looks* pleasant is of no value if it does not enable the rider to influence his horse in a correct and sensitive way.

INFLUENCES OF THE WEIGHT

Seat with equal distribution of the weight. Every body, whatever its shape or form, has a centre of gravity. If the centre of gravity is supported, the body is stable. The vertical line going through the centre of gravity is called the line of gravity. Each body has only one centre of gravity and there is only one vertical line that can be drawn through it at any instant. A body can, of course, be supported at several points, as, for instance, a table (or a horse) by its four legs, or a rider, whose weight rests on the crotch and the two pelvic bones (three points). If the centre of gravity is supported, then, as we have said before, the body is stable; if it is not supported the body must topple over. If a body changes its outline or form (as a human body does whenever its owner moves) it also changes the position of its centre of gravity. The centre of gravity may even be outside the body's mass, as is the case with rings, hollow balls, cups, or with a rider in the racing or jumping seat.

A rider sitting straight on his horse sits in such a position that his centre of gravity is more or less vertically above the horse's centre of gravity. His line of gravity, to all practical intents and purposes, coincides with that of the horse. This is assuming, of course, that the horse is resting on all four legs, in a normal position and on level ground. (See Fig. 9.)

Each movement of the horse (stretching his neck or lifting his head), each lateral flexion to the left or to the right, shifts his centre of gravity to a certain extent. And the rider must always bring his centre of gravity into co-ordination with the horse's, that is to say, he must balance himself.

This sounds like the greyest theory, yet it is the basis of all feel. On it depends all harmony and that which we ordinarily call 'a rider's balanced seat'.

In this way, the horse can deal best with the rider's weight and the rider again can best dispose of his horse's powers. In the same way, a porter carries a trunk on his back and in the

3

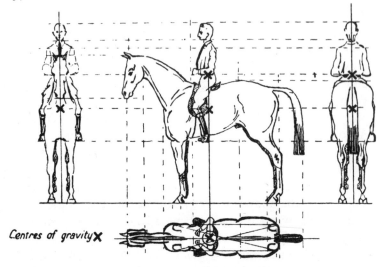

Centres of gravity ✗

Fig. 9. SEAT IN EQUILIBRIUM

same way, a juggler goes through his tricks, where the laws
of balance can be studied par excellence. (Fig. 10.)

Balance during the forward movement. When a horse moves

Fig. 10. THE JUGGLER

forward the rider must, according to the horse's speed, move
his centre of gravity forward to such an extent that it is placed
in front of the horse's centre of gravity; provided always that he

wants to keep in the saddle by mere balance. This is called 'going with the horse' or 'following the horse' (see p. 12). If the rider 'stays behind' the movement of his horse he will only be carried along if he 'cramps on'. The rider must fulfil two conditions, those of: (a) bringing his own centre of gravity into co-ordination with that of the horse, and (b) placing his seat upon three points of support.

These two requirements do not always go well together. At the forward movement the centre of gravity can only be shifted forward by a forward inclination of the trunk; this necessitates lifting the pelvic bones out of the saddle. The rider then sits only on the crotch, possibly stands in the stirrups and 'clamps' with the upper legs ('crotch seat').

In slow or shortened gaits (walk —collected trot—collected canter), this contradiction is not so evident; nevertheless it can be felt distinctly or else the beginner would have no difficulties in 'going with the horse'. The critical moment is always the beginning of a movement when the rider, owing to his inertia, has a tendency to topple over backward.

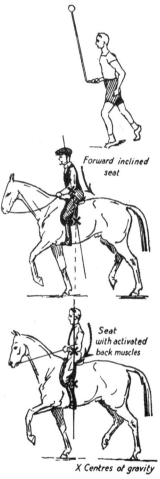

Forward inclined seat

Seat with activated back muscles

X Centres of gravity

Fig. 11. THE CROTCH SEAT (FORWARD INCLINED)

Therefore, the aids for walking on (see p. 113) as also, in general, every 'urging on', must needs be identical with the

principle of the bracing of the back and the thigh pressure by
which the rider 'sticks to the saddle' and 'follows the horse's
movements'. The rider who is pressing his horse forward, is,
as I have said before, sucking himself on with legs and loins,
pushing his buttocks and his whole centre of gravity well
forward. This results in a
very close contact with the
horse and, at the same time,
enables the rider to avoid
bumping in the saddle and
'being left behind'. He
remains firmly seated on
the three points; he can at
any time influence his
horse, stop, turn, or urge
him on. He will also re-
main in the saddle if the
horse 'pecks' and in the case
of a sudden stop or startle
can push him forward; in
short—he can control his
horse.

THE AMERICAN RACING SEAT

A rider using the 'crotch
seat', more or less 'floating'
on top of the horse, has
no fast grip in his seat; he
must needs fall forward
whenever the horse

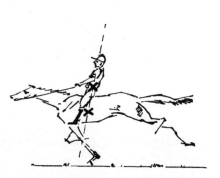

THE 'CONVENTIONAL' RACING SEAT
USED UNTIL APPROX. A.D. 1900

Fig. 12.

stumbles or stops short and, before making any single influence,
he must first 'sit down'.

At the fast paces the discrepancy between the requirement to
sit on three points and the necessity to bring one's own centre
of gravity into harmony with the horse's, becomes more and
more acute. At the extended trot, this ultimately leads to an
obligation on the rider to 'post', for he can no longer follow the

THE 'ITALIAN' SEAT

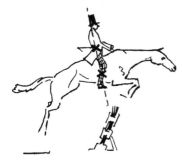

THE OLD JUMPING SEAT
USED UNTIL 1910

AND : 'IF HE HADN'T HUNG
ON FOR LIFE !'

Fig. 13.

movement. At the gallop, the rider must lean right forward into the movement. And when going still faster—as in racing, or jumping—the rider must finally abandon the seat in the saddle altogether, 'following the horse's movements' being impossible and the attempt to do so only hampering. In these cases the rider finds his support in his knees, in shorter stirrups, and in resting his hands on the horse's neck. (See p. 170.)

The 'American racing seat' therefore in no way contradicts the requirements of the classical art of riding, whereas the old racing seat, out of sheer thoughtless over-estimation of a 'correct' appearance, defied all laws of balance.

The 'Italian' jumping seat, likewise, is not an exaggeration, but merely the outcome of zealous attempts to establish harmony, which, after all, is the cardinal aim of the classical art of riding.

Influence of the weight forward and backward. While the forward movement of the horse requires the rider to adapt himself to this movement, the rider, on the other hand, cannot exert any appreciable influences upon the horse by moving his centre of gravity forward or backward.

The reason for this is, that the rider, in leaning forward or backward abandons the solid basis of his seat on the crotch and the pelvis, and involuntarily alters the influence of his back and legs. The alteration of these influences has, of course, consequences, and these are deceiving as to the effect of shifting the weight.

One would think that leaning the body forward would have an urging-on effect upon the horse. Yet this is not so. And although it is necessary to lean the body forward in a faster movement, one cannot produce this fast movement by leaning the body forward. One would also suppose that leaning the body backward and thus shifting the centre of gravity towards the rear should have a restraining effect upon the horse, but it very often produces just the opposite result! It urges him on, because it is often accompanied by a bracing of the back-muscles. Leaning the body backwards, however, has in itself no urging effect as it is not identical with 'bracing the back'.

Balance at the side movements. Whenever a horse bends, flexes, or turns to the right or to the left, it shifts to a greater or lesser extent, according to the degree of the flexion, its centre of gravity. When turning at a fast gait, an additional inclination, that is, a lean-to, is added to counteract the centrifugal force. If the rider wants to remain 'balanced' he must accordingly shift his centre of gravity sideways. This is made easier by the fact that the inner back-muscles of the horse (those on the side nearer to the imaginary centre of the turn) become a little flatter when he bends or flexes. Through this circumstance the rider who is sticking close to the saddle will automatically be seated by the horse towards the inside. If he assists this movement by firmly pressing down the heel on the side towards which he wants to shift his weight, he will put more weight upon the inner pelvic bone. The feel for this seat is acquired in the first few lessons, when the rider begins to notice that while passing a corner he has a tendency to slip off the saddle towards the outside of the corner unless he leans-to like a bicycle rider.

It would, however, be entirely wrong to assume that this can be achieved by deliberately *leaning* the body in the required direction. This invariably results in a collapse at the hip, producing just the opposite effect.

If the rider wants to remain in harmony with his horse, and if he wants to retain a continuous subtle contact with legs and reins he must, according to the flexion of the horse's body:

> remain with his hips parallel to the hips of the horse, and with his shoulders parallel to the shoulders of the horse.

The legs direct the hindquarters and assume quite automatically a correct position if they remain in contact with the horse's body: the inner leg at the girth, the outer leg about a hand to the rear of the girth.

The rider's hands partake in the slight twist of the shoulders in relation to the hips. The inner hand comes slightly backward and the outer hand slightly forward, according to the flexion of the horse. Thus the rider always has the horse's neck straight in front of him and, when superficially looked at, will yet appear to sit perfectly straight. (See Fig. 14.)

The rider can easily find out for himself whether he has acquired a 'laterally balanced seat', by dropping the stirrups at a turn and stretching his lower legs away from the horse. If he slips towards the outside his seat is bad.

Influence of the weight sideways. The area of support of the horse is considerably smaller from right to left than from front to rear. Consequently, if the rider's line of gravity coincides with that of the horse, the latter will at once feel the slightest lateral displacement of the rider's centre of gravity. By moving his own centre of gravity the rider can therefore cause the horse to shift his centre of gravity. This is what is meant by 'influence of the weight'. These influences too, if exerted in the right way, are hardly perceptible to the unskilled observer, and every exaggeration is a mistake. 'The horse assumes the position[1] which his rider assumes.' The reverse of this sentence, 'the rider must assume the position of his horse', also is true for the seat and the behaviour of the rider at all turns or changes of direction and at the canter. This reciprocal action, resulting from a feel of co-ordination between rider and horse, is the source of all harmony. On it are based to a large extent the natural aids and the possibility of riding a horse with a minimum amount of effort. For this reason the ability and capability of a high-school rider does not decrease with age but, on the contrary, increases. (See Plate 2.)

A lateral displacement of the weight towards the right or towards the left causes the horse either to deviate from his straight course or to flex (bend) in that direction, according to the manner in which back, reins, and legs simultaneously exert their influences.

But it cannot be said too often that any displacement of the weight must be so slight that the rider appears to the untrained eye to be sitting almost straight. The greatest care must be taken not to exaggerate; if a lateral displacement of the weight can distinctly be *seen* it is exaggerated and the rider has a bad seat.

INFLUENCES OF THE REINS

Generally much too much is said of 'hands', meaning 'influences of the reins'. Most riders are inclined to do far too much with their hands, and all men believe themselves to be fairly clever with their hands, because they know how to use them in daily life. Many people cannot even talk without their hands.

---

[1] 'Position' denotes here direction, i.e. the position which the horse must assume in order to execute correct *manège* figures. THE TRANSLATOR.

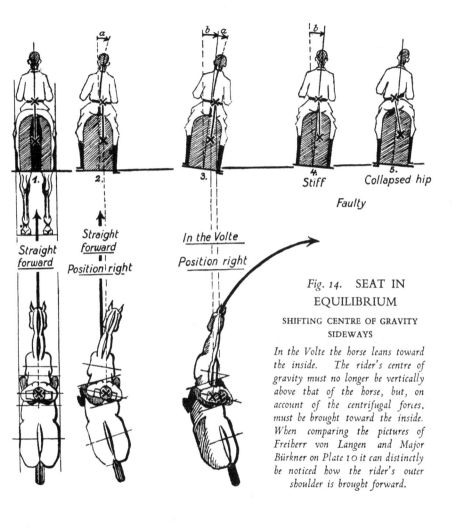

1. Straight forward

2. Straight forward
Position right

3. In the Volte
Position right

4. Stiff

5. Collapsed hip

Faulty

Fig. 14. SEAT IN EQUILIBRIUM

SHIFTING CENTRE OF GRAVITY SIDEWAYS

In the Volte the horse leans toward the inside. The rider's centre of gravity must no longer be vertically above that of the horse, but, on account of the centrifugal forces, must be brought toward the inside. When comparing the pictures of Freiherr von Langen and Major Bürkner on Plate 10 it can distinctly be noticed how the rider's outer shoulder is brought forward.

We often hear of a rider that he 'has good hands'. The hands of a rider can only be 'good' if they are steady. This is only possible if the rider sits quiet in the saddle, glued to it, as it were, and if he knows how to brace his back to follow the movements of the horse, and if he, moreover, knows how to drive the horse with his legs 'into' his hands, i.e. on to the bit. Therefore, one should not speak first of his 'hands', but rather of all the rest.

True, the influences of the hands are important, but not nearly as important as is generally believed. The less the hands are used the more perfect the riding. In forceful action of the hands lies a great danger.

This explains the fact that women, who are mostly weaker than men, have as a rule better 'hands' than their masculine colleagues, who are all too prone to use their strength.

If the rider wants to make independent use of his hands he can only do so if they remain independent of the vibrations and shakings to which the body is subject. This necessitates that muscles and joints of upper and lower arm be completely relaxed and supple.

With a beginner it is best to use side reins on the horse and to give the rider no reins at all until he has learned 'to balance'. When he has learned that, he will no longer have any reason to make his arms stiff. With rigid arms most riders, if we may say so, 'beat time' as they are being bumped or tossed by the horse. The arms, however, should not flop about uncontrolled; they must make a counter-movement, as it were, in order to remain steady, even if the body is moving by force of the horse's motion. They must be so steady that the horse is not jabbed in the mouth, so steady that at the trot they could hold a glass of water without spilling a drop. This is not meant as a joke, but should actually be tried out by every rider.

If a rider wants to acquire steady hands while his body is moving he must, in recognition of this difficulty, endeavour to get control over his hands. The easiest way consciously to keep

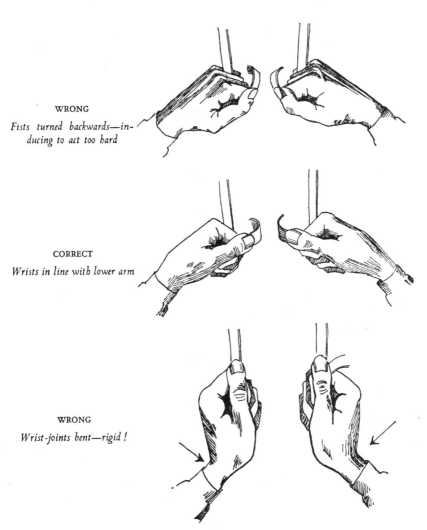

WRONG

Fists turned backwards—inducing to act too hard

CORRECT

Wrists in line with lower arm

WRONG

Wrist-joints bent—rigid!

Fig. 15. POSITION OF HANDS

the hands steady is to keep them busy. But by anxiously paying attention to the steadiness of the hands one is apt to relapse
into the first mistake, that of making the arms rigid. It is a
good practice to take a whip or a switch in each hand and hold
them vertical, so that one can see by their movements how
steady the hands are. It will help to further steadiness of
the hands and will help to develop the feel for it. The
whip or riding stick as a means of testing the hands should be
used as often as possible, even at an advanced stage. Riders
with really steady hands are very, very rare indeed.

The hands are not necessarily bound to a certain position;
but unless there is a special reason to the contrary they rest close
together in front of the body (see Fig. 15), just as high and as
close to the body as will allow them at any time to 'give' or to
go forward, without forcing the rider to alter his seat.

The lower arms form approximately a right angle with the
upper arms so that by extending the elbows the reins are made
to 'give'. The upper arms hang down loosely; they must not
be stretched away nor must they be pressed to the body. The
elbows should therefore not cling to the body as this produces
a stiff and artificial position.

The hips should constantly seek contact with the lower arms.
This produces what we call a 'rounded seat'. To attain it,
however, the arms should not be drawn up to the body, but,
on the contrary, the body drawn up to the arms. This is
effected in such a way that the urging legs drive the horse
against the bit, and the rider's body is, so to speak, brought up
to his lower arms. (See Plate 4.)

All influences of the reins must, of course, be exerted with
feel, which is only possible if there is always a constant, soft
contact between the hands and the horse's mouth. If the reins
are hanging slack it is impossible to act with them quickly,
sensitively and with feel. The horse must needs be jerked at
the mouth.

Rein influences therefore require as the foremost condition

that the horse be 'driven into the aids', meaning that one must not first act with the reins but must first 'influence' with back and legs (see paragraph, 'putting the horse to the aids', p. 65). The influences of the reins consist in:

(1) 'Giving', with both reins or with one rein, by twisting or screwing the fist or by slightly going forward with both hands and arms.

(2) 'Tightening' both reins or one rein by twisting or screwing the fist in order to shorten the reins by fractions of inches, but never by moving the arms as for an actual 'pull', because the horse is always stronger and in a tug-of-war will always win. Beware, *homo sapiens*, and never try it !

(3) 'Passively maintaining' tension on both reins or unilaterally, the fists remaining perfectly still.

An attempt to try out rein action independently of other influences would result in:

(1) the reins hanging slack when one is trying to make them 'give', which must not occur and can be prevented only by driving influences;

(2) one's having to pull at the reins in order to 'tighten' them, which should not occur either and can be prevented only by driving influences;

(3) Nothing—when trying out the passive maintaining of tension. And this is the most difficult and most important: to remain passive with one or both reins while back and legs drive the horse forward.

Rein control can, therefore, only be learned on the living horse which simultaneously reacts to rein-, back-, and leg-influences.

(a) Bilateral or equal rein effects on both sides, such as 'giving,' 'tightening', or 'passive tension' in both

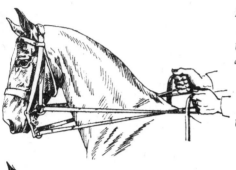

Fig. 16. MILITARY METHOD OF HOLDING THE REINS

Used in Germany, France, Sweden, Austria; also recognized method for Olympic Games.

I

DIVIDED REINS

Used by civilians; in exceptional cases also by the cavalry

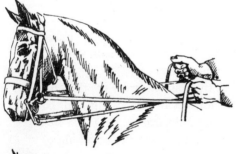

2

REINS IN ONE HAND

in front of body

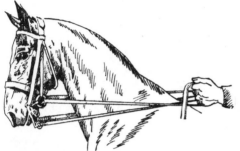

3

DIVIDED SNAFFLE REINS

Basic military method; left hand in centre and in front of body, right hand close to it in front of right hip

4

TAUT CURB REINS

Method for Trooping, etc.

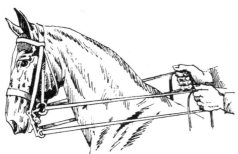

Fig. 17.
FILLIS METHOD

(Also called French method—not invented by James Fillis, but made popular by him. Not used in the French Army)

5

DIVIDED REINS

Basic position of this method

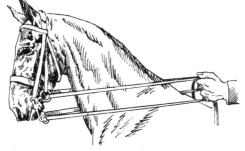

6

REINS IN ONE HAND

in front of body

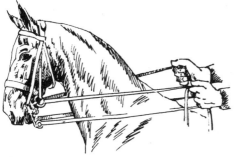

7

DIVIDED SNAFFLE REINS
seldom used
Left hand in front of centre of body, right hand close to it in front of right hip

8

ANOTHER TYPE OF 'DIVIDED REINS'

often used
Left hand with curb reins in front of centre of body, right hand with snaffle reins exactly above left hand

reins, is learned in walking on, trotting on, and halting (see Lessons, p. 113). The most critical test as to the worst mistake, that is, 'pulling at the reins', is the lesson for the 'rein back'. (See p. 141.)

(b) Unilateral rein effect, that is, different effects with the off and near reins (tightening the one and remaining passive with the other, or remaining passive with the one and 'giving' with the other), can best be learned in turns, especially at the halt, such as 'pivot on the shoulders' and 'pivot on the haunches'. These lessons, particularly the 'pivot on the haunches' are therefore of considerable importance in the training of the rider; not simply for the sake of the exercise, but in order to teach him the feel of the way in which the several influences must harmoniously co-operate and how they influence the horse.

Unilateral or different rein effects are required for every turn, for all lateral flexions and for the canter. If the rider wants to execute these lessons in the forward movement he must first acquire at the halt a conception of the consequences of these 'aids'.

The movements of the hands for obtaining 'rein effects' depend on the bridle and the manner in which the reins are held.

Civil riders mostly use 'divided reins' as it is easier to learn with them. Their advantage is that the softer snaffle rein always comes into play first and the more severe curb rein only secondarily. This is a real blessing, since most riders, as has been said before, are prone to do too much with their hands.

(1) *The military method* requires a considerably longer training and much more practice. Since the left hand should be right in the middle and in front of the body and the right hand approximately in front of the right hip, there is a tendency

towards a one-sided position. It is not possible to keep both hands in front of the body because the curb reins would act askew. This, quite naturally, is the cause of a great number of mistakes. The military method of holding the reins is necessary in the Army because the right arm must be ready at any moment to grasp a weapon.

From a purely riding point of view, it is advisable with the military method to divide the reins as soon as difficulties arise, in order to avoid the danger of faulty unilateral influences.

The only advantage of the military method is the refinement of the rein effects. The rider is compelled to rely exclusively on his left hand; the left hand is generally the weaker hand. Moreover, the necessity of using one hand only tends to make the rider put less effort into it, and therefore leads to greater subtlety.

In tournaments competitors usually use the military method.

(2) *The Fillis method* allows of still more subtle influences, as the difference of the rein effects, e.g. the more erecting effect of the snaffle, and the more collecting effect of the curb, is a more pronounced one.

A person who is used to the military method has difficulties when first trying the Fillis method, because the movements of the fists must needs be different on account of the different positions of the snaffle and curb reins. Each twist of the hands in such a direction that the little fingers are raised towards the chest would have a very strong effect on the curb reins which are lying below. It is therefore necessary for the rider to get rid of this movement—if he can ! And as this is almost impossible—to those used to the other method of holding the reins—this type of rein control usually results in much too heavy hands.

The rein position indicated in Fig. 18 on the next page, is not practical as it is an inducement to act with the whole arm instead of just turning or twisting the fist. (See also Fig. 15 above.)

4

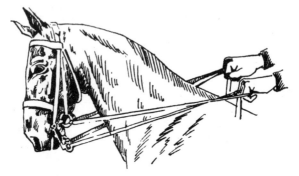

Fig. 18. 'ENGLISH' POSITION OF REINS

There are various methods of starting beginners. In most cases it is best to let them ride first with a snaffle, and later on, when a certain amount of practice has been acquired, with curb reins.

(*a*) Riding with a snaffle is easier because the snaffle reins are simpler to hold, and therefore easier to understand.

(*b*) Riding with the curb reins has the advantage that most horses are more collected in them and have softer paces (as they would be if side reins were used) and therefore toss a little less.

The most difficult part about rein control is the circumstance that rein influences must always be implemented with a minimum of effort and never independently for themselves alone. Back, leg and weight influences should always predominate because every movement on horseback should result from 'going forward', from the urging and driving influences, just as motor and propeller are indispensable for aircraft.

The curb can hurt the horse more than the snaffle, because it acts as a lever. Young horses and badly schooled ones, or horses which are to be 'put to the aids' should therefore be ridden on a plain snaffle. Or one can eliminate the curb action with a double bridle by just letting the curb reins hang down. This course should also be taken in emergencies, if a horse bucks or shies or refuses to jump, etc. A horse will gain confidence much more quickly in the plain snaffle because its action is softer. However, for finishing an advanced dressage the curb is indispensable.

The movements which the hands execute for the purposes of rein influences, and about which most riding instructors talk too much, must at all times be limited to slight and hardly perceptible twists of the fists. All aids—even the one for turning—should mainly result from the seat. This twist, either to 'give' with the rein or to take it up, is very, very slight and can easily be learned.

It is utterly wrong to attempt a turn, or any change of direction, by rein influences alone, or mainly by rein influences. This is 'driving' but not riding, and in order to emphasize the fact that the hand movements are negligibly small we do not describe them at all.

In the end, controlling the reins must be more or less a reflex movement, the execution of which should require just as little thought as the leg actions.

Influences of the Back

Influences of the back can only be exerted by the rider in conjunction with his legs, just the same as he can only tilt the stool through a back-muscle action (see p. 18) if he braces his feet on the floor. As soon as he lifts his feet off the ground when sitting on the stool, or stretches his legs away from the horse, he cannot exert a proper influence. The activity of the muscles for bracing the back is discussed on p. 15. The movement itself is not difficult, but it is not easy to make its application understood.

Back-muscle action runs through the whole of the science of equitation. The back is always the connexion or the bridge between legs and reins. The influences exerted by the legs and the reins can only be in harmony if a simultaneous action of the back effects an intimate connexion between them. The back, so to say, beats time and gives the command for the aid, just as if it said: 'now!' Not one of the influences must be omitted or must come too late, or the horse would not understand the aid. It is therefore impossible to try the 'influences of the back' separately and independently.

If a rider, on a well-schooled horse, is bracing his back while having a good contact with his legs and if the reins simultaneously:

give—the horse will move on (see Plate 4 centre),
do not give—the horse will stop (see Plate 4 below).

The difference in the effect is therefore not dependent on the action of the back but only on the reins. *The action of the back in both cases is the same.* With a less perfect horse an additional pressure of both legs will be required, which, however, must set in simultaneously with the action of the back and the action of the hands.

If the rider does not at the walk or at the halt, brace his back, he requires a much stronger pressure of the legs. The finer and more advanced the riding, the greater the importance attributable to the effect of the back action.

Nervous and timid horses, highly-strung thoroughbreds, and also most English-bred horses, very strongly resent crude aids and often strike if the rider does not use tact and discretion in his 'influences'.

This is explained by the fact that the aids will only be understood by the horse as 'aids', and will only then have an harmonious effect, if they are actually given in full harmony with the horse, that is, if the two living beings, man and mount, are in perfect co-ordination at the moment the aids are given, or in other words, if the rider is 'glued' to the saddle.[1]

[1] Even the most expert waiter must learn to juggle plates or dishes in a dining-car. If he has no feel for balance or for 'going with the movement' of the swaying carriage he will most probably 'spill the beans'.

If the rider at the moment of applying the aids is left behind, there can be no question of well-measured aids in full harmony and all the influences he wants to exert must needs result in more or less involuntary jabs and jerks. Harmony, sticking to the saddle and 'going with the horse' can only be effected by bracing the back. (See pp. 12, 35.)

A rider who does not master this back-muscle action or who, despite years of practice does not believe in its effect, had better try it on a really well-schooled horse; he will quickly reconsider his opinion and he will, no doubt, be able to improve his feel and his influencing powers.

When riding 'in position', at every turn, and at the canter, the rider must push the inner pelvic bone and hip forward. That is easy to say, but the rider who does not know how to do it will hardly derive any benefit from his instructor's advice, 'inner hip forward!' This exercise has been discussed on p. 19.

If there is a perfect harmony between rider and horse, it is sufficient for the former to brace his back unilaterally (i.e. push one pelvic bone and the hip on the same side forward) in connection with a slight displacement of weight, in order to let the horse canter on, change legs, or turn.

It is important and necessary that the rider learn as early as possible the influences of the back, so that he does not acquire a wrong idea about giving aids of which it is difficult later on to get rid.

Children easily learn on a swing how to make use of their back-muscles. Why then should a rider, who must know this action from childhood, not be in a position to make use of it! In the first riding lessons he will immediately get a better understanding for the proper seat and he will at once know what the instructor means by asking him to push his buttocks well forward in the saddle.

'Wipe the saddle from back to front!' (What a thought!) 'Body backward!' 'Chest forward!' The instructor, in order to make himself understood, should not resort to such

erroneous corrections, which do not remove the cause of the
mistake. They only lead to further mystifying comments,
such as: 'Imagine you want to lean against the back of a chair—
as if the saddle had a back to it !' Certainly, the rider should
not sit 'leaning forward', but he can only avoid this by learning
to 'brace his back' and not by trying to execute commands
like 'Body backward, chest forward'. Such 'corrections' do
not help him, they only make him stiff.

HOW DOES THE RIDER LEARN TO SCHOOL A HORSE?

Only practical school work will enable a rider to acquire
this art. When putting a last polish on the education of young
riders, who should receive their training on well-schooled
horses, one should work as if it was not a case of training the
rider, but the horse. Rider and horse must educate each
other. Each lesson which is devoted to the making of a horse
should also be an education for the rider, and vice versa.
Eventually it will hardly be possible to tell the difference
between lessons in which the horse is the learning party and
those in which the rider is the pupil.

According to his temper and his conformation each horse
provides a new task for the rider and is a new experience for
him. 'Feel' is everything, and it is a long, long way to perfection and harmony between man and mount.

The 'Campagne School' comprises the whole range of lessons
which serve the purpose of controlling the horse across country.

The 'High School' comprises all those lessons which, on a
natural basis, can be taught the horse from the saddle. In
general it signifies such exercises as changing legs at the canter
(flying changes), Piaffer, Passage, Levade (Pesade) and
Pirouettes at the canter. All other gaits, and unnatural movements which have to be taught the horse in artificial ways or
by means of special appliances, belong neither to the High
School nor to the Campagne School.

II

THE SCHOOLING OF THE HORSE

PSYCHOLOGY OF THE HORSE

THE HORSE is very good natured, very friendly towards man, and much more sensitive than is generally assumed. He is very receptive to patting and fondling, and besides possessing a marvellous memory, has an exceedingly well-developed sense of locality. He very quickly acquires habits and firmly sticks to them. On the other hand, he is slower and much less intelligent than a dog, and, being timid, can easily be frightened by rough handling or punishment.

It is absolutely essential that the rider know all these qualities, which, of course, are differently developed in every animal. In the first place, one should make full use of his docility, his memory and his peculiar persistence in sticking to certain habits. And always one must bear in mind that the horse is exceedingly sensitive, that he is a living being with a psychology all his own and that one can never treat him like a machine.

Every difficulty that arises in riding has its special cause; the same difficulties, however, can have various causes. If one does not fully recognize the latter fact—and that is the most difficult part about it—one will never be in a position to avoid awkward consequences. A horse is easily frightened and full of fear, much more so than man. Fear or fright are the causes for quite a number of his sudden actions, such as stopping short, shying, jumping sideways, bolting and rearing, and for even minor signs of restiveness such as nappy steps, throwing the head about, twisting the tail, and so on. One must always behave like a good schoolteacher, bearing in

55

mind the very low intelligence of the horse. Such difficulties should never be attributed to disobedience ('The beast doesn't want to !' etc.), but the cause should first of all and always be looked for in the rider. Quiet reflection and patience will have better results than punishment, which the horse often does not understand, often indeed *cannot* understand, and which in any case frequently only intimidates him still more.

Good riding requires of the rider that he try continuously to 'feel' into the feelings and thoughts of his horse. It is only from the point of view of the horse that he can understand whether the meaning of certain aids or influences has been grasped or not.

For this reason it is also imperative to bear in mind the very strong gregarious instinct of the horse. Otherwise this natural disposition will lead to difficulties and so-called 'bad habits'. It cannot be helped that horses are always tending towards other horses and that they invariably prefer to go in company. The rider must pay attention to this and must reckon with it. The gregarious instinct can be very useful in training. For jumping lessons, for instance, it is well to arrange that the horse always sees one or more horses on the other side of the fence, and it is also of advantage to get a lead over the fence by some other horse. All horses jump far better in company, as can be seen in the hunting field.

Timid and shy horses will pass unfamiliar objects much more readily if accompanied by other horses. If a horse shies, for instance, in front of an automobile or a steam-roller he will very quickly get used to it if another horse is leading the way past the vehicle. A clever rider will therefore always see that he can 'hang on to others'. Yet, one should not call this 'clever', but rather 'psychologically correct' and 'right'. The rider's wish to carry out his will against the fear of the horse is, psychologically, nonsense if he has not the power to do it.

In training a horse over jumps, it will be of advantage to start him jumping towards the stable and not away from it.

In the covered school, one should jump him towards the exit and not away from it. One should also be aware of the fact that frequent halts or stops in the covered school close to the entrance will cause the horse to get 'sticky' near the door and to sidle in the direction of the stable. Likewise, a horse will acquire the habit of hurrying towards the stable if, in going home and coming near the stable, the rider habitually throws away the reins and leaves the horse to pick his own way to the stable. The horse will very quickly fall into this habit, with the result that when the rider tries one day to take up the reins and, instead of going to the stable, continue the ride, the horse will object and may refuse to walk away from the stable. The reason for this, however, is not a 'bad habit' of the horse, but the fact that the rider did not take into calculation the psychology of his mount when he first adopted the casual practice of letting the animal find its own way to the stable.

THE PURPOSE OF SCHOOLING

The purpose of schooling a horse is to be able to get about on him and to go wherever one wants with a minimum of exertion and effort for the rider and with a maximum of ease and therefore preservation for the horse. The schooling which the horse gets for this purpose is called 'dressage'. It comprises the gymnastic training of the horse to maximum efficiency and education to obedience.

Although the purpose of all dressage seems to be such a simple and general one, the practical ends which the riders want to attain and the work which they require from their horses are varied. Different results, however, cannot be reached by the same method; this means that one cannot always follow the same course of training. Yet, very often, different ways are called different 'methods' although, on proper investigation, we find that they are all based on the same principles and that they supplement rather than contradict each other. It is necessary to explain this more fully because often there arise disputes, doubts, and errors if the ultimate end which it is desired to attain is forgotten.

If there is perfect harmony between rider and horse it is sufficient for the former to brace his loins unilaterally (i.e. push one pelvic bone or the hip on the same side forward) in connexion with a slight displacement of weight, in order to let the horse canter on, change legs, or turn.

(a) *The Soldier.* Cavalry horses must be trained to suit many riders and a variety of purposes. They must go in formation or singly many hours a day across country, sometimes under very difficult circumstances and over obstacles of all kinds. For economic reasons many thousands of these horses must be kept fit to give useful service for a long time. In their case a thorough education in obedience, physical dressage, cross-country riding and jumping is therefore necessary.

(b) *The School Rider.* In order to set a standard of achievement for correct dressage and to show which methods give the best results, certain riding schools aim at peak performances. The military riding schools at Hanover (Germany), Saumur (France) and Weedon (England), are based on practical military riding; the 'Imperial Spanish Riding School' in Vienna (Austria) (see Plate 5), cultivates the proper High School (Haute École) riding without paying very much attention to its usefulness for cross-country purposes.

(c) *The Show Rider* who wants to get prizes in dressage and utility tests must train his horse according to the principles of school riding. Before attaining his goal, the blue rosette, he has ample opportunity to have his work as well as his mount examined and judged in the various tests. It then often happens that in an attempt to get as high a mark as possible he lets himself be tempted to show more than he can actually manage.

(d) *The 'Pleasure Rider'* wants to move about in all gaits as comfortably as possible. The horse must be easy to turn and to stop, and must have a nice short canter. He therefore requires a very obedient animal, not necessarily possessed of great efficiency and endurance. As such riders usually like to give a pleasant display, the horse should bridle well and should therefore be well trained.

(e) The *Bailiff* or *Farm-surveyor* needs a good-natured, very hardy and untiring horse for his daily ride over the estate or farm, one that will not shy and will stand still without reins, even near a threshing machine. For this purpose older horses with not too much temper are suitable. This type of rider does not require highly developed efficiency, speed or jumping power, nor is a very thorough schooling of importance.

(f) For *Hunting Men*, a horse must be able to gallop, he must be a 'good lepper', and he must be untiring. He must be fast enough for it to be unnecessary for one to be constantly 'riding him'; and he must not—and this is perhaps still more important—be a puller. With the hunter, therefore, it is more innate qualities than training or dressage that is required.

(g) The *Show Jumping Rider* requires an animal of particular talent. Top performances can only be obtained on horses with a natural talent for jumping and whose talent has been developed to the utmost point of efficiency by a special training. Such horses must also be very handy in order to be quick around bends over a difficult course, and they must therefore be very well trained to obey the aids. This, unfortunately, is often neglected !

(h) The *Race Rider* requires the fastest horse. From a riding point of view he requires little schooling. Breed and pedigree are the important points and, later on, his proper training.

(i) The *Circus Rider* wants to show to a wide lay public things similar to the high-school rider. For him, next to profits, complete harmony between rider and horse are not as important (although he rather appreciates it) as the ability to show to a public which does not understand too much of riding, a number of effective and brilliant tricks and movements.

Since these horses have not to be ridden across country, these trick effects can be obtained by special training much more quickly than by a comprehensive course of dressage.

The purposes described above dictate the particular method to be adopted for the schooling of any horse. Often it will be necessary, if one wants to save time and labour, to rest content with a lesser degree of obedience and training.

The military, the show rider and the school rider depend largely on 'dressage' methods for their purposes.

The hack, the farm inspector's cob and the hunter can do with a little less.

The show jumper, the racehorse and the circus 'steed', must go through their own particular and special training.

For all of them, however, the principles of schooling are unquestionably useful. Where time and good riders are available, proper schooling and dressage can only be of advantage to the horse whatever his destination, besides providing great pleasure to the eventual owner and rider. If the schooling, however, is done in haste and without careful planning—and this, unfortunately, is more often than not the case—it does more harm than good. The difficulties lie in recognizing whether the schooling is carried on correctly or not.

PRINCIPAL VIEWS ON SCHOOLING

It is generally assumed that in the course of centuries the basic views on schooling horses have undergone considerable changes and that they differ widely in the various countries of the world. One hears talk of the 'classical art of riding', and of a 'German' and a 'Roman school'.

The 'classical art of riding' does not consist of single or independent lessons or dogmas, any more than the 'Baroque' or 'Renaissance' styles consist of certain ornaments or architectural lines. It represents an undivided entity, comprising all means and ends of the art of riding. The 'classical art of riding' can best be defined as the method that aims at obtaining perfect harmony between rider and horse in a natural way and in full consideration of the psychology of the horse. Everything which is contrary to nature, all artificiality or artificial gaits, are outside the classical art of riding.

The 'German' and the 'Roman' schools are both based on this same conception. They are closely related to each other. The difference between them lies simply in the difference of temper and character of the two nations. The German is more thorough and indulges more in theories, the Frenchman is much lighter and has an outspoken sense for elegance.

The English, on the whole, have not really a systematically developed system of schooling. They rely on the excellent character of their horses.

The 'Italian' method does not attach much importance to dressage. It argues that the best way of preparing a horse for cross-country work is a thorough development of his jumping capabilities.

There are always differences of opinion in every field. Expert lawyers or medical men are very seldom entirely in agreement. Why should riders be expected to be more so, when the disputes in their subject are not even matters of definite fact, as they are, for instance, in mathematical problems, but matters of feeling, temper, and talent of rider, horse and instructor, these variable components being of decisive importance ? The difficulty in coming to an agreement is very often caused by the fact that the parties do not even adopt a common basis from which to proceed. It is also an unfortunate circumstance that descriptive words, slogans and *termini technici* are used, the dictionary meaning of which may well be definite, but the conceptions of which held by the contending parties vary widely.

Yet, there does exist one fundamental principle dating from the time of Xenophon, who wrote the oldest known riding instructions, and that is: that the procedure in the dressage must be determined by the end to be attained, by the time available for the training, by the horse to be schooled and by the abilities, knowledge and temper of the riders who are to do the schooling.

PROCEDURE IN SCHOOLING

Schooling can be divided into three distinct stages:

First stage:

The green horse is backed, i.e. it is made accustomed to the weight of the rider.

Second stage:

The horse is 'put to the aids'.

Third stage:

The horse thus 'put to the aids' is (a) educated to obedience, (b) trained.

I. The first stage must be gone through by every horse which is to be used as a mount of any kind.

II. The second stage should also be applied to almost any riding horse. It is necessary to make the animal acquainted with the aids before asking him to obey them. If a horse is neatly and properly 'put to the aids' he is well prepared for any purpose for which he may later be required. Lack of knowledge is very often the cause of many breaches of this rule.

III. The third stage comprises the dressage proper. Its place is taken by certain special trainings if the horse is used for other purposes. The end of the second stage is therefore the parting of the ways in the various types of training.

FIRST STAGE OF SCHOOLING

MAKING THE GREEN HORSE ACQUAINTED WITH THE UNACCUSTOMED WEIGHT OF THE RIDER

A horse which has not yet been backed, naturally finds the weight of the rider on his back a more or less disagreeable encumbrance. The natural timidity of the horse will, moreover, produce a certain fear, all the more so in proportion to the crudeness with which the rider goes about the job. In the beginning, when trying to put a saddle on, the voice and a lot of patting or 'making much of him' must be used to induce quietness and confidence. The actual words are of no importance; it is the tone of the voice that counts. Each mistake, each carelessness, will have grave consequences owing to the remarkable memory and natural timidity and shyness of the horse. The horse should, therefore, be saddled in his most familiar surroundings, that is, in his stall or loose-box. It is best if the rider does this himself, while the groom who regularly 'does the horse' gives him a good patting on the neck.

After saddling, it is advisable first of all to lunge the horse (see p. 183), particularly if he shows tenseness in the back-muscles or short, nappy steps when he comes out of the stable. It would be a mistake to mount such a horse immediately. It is also advisable to remedy tenseness by lunging if it appears later on after the horse has been mounted. The more carefully and the slower one proceeds at the beginning, the better and faster will be the progress later on.

Each time one mounts the horse it should be done with the utmost care and caution. At first he should always be held by a stable lad or whoever else is available. The helper must be instructed to pat the horse on the neck during the mounting, and to talk to him quietly. He should then lead him on immediately after the rider is in the saddle. Rash and hasty movements frighten a horse.

Good-tempered horses will quickly get accustomed to the weight of the rider if only he goes about it fairly cleverly. They will soon regain their balance, which, of course, will have been disturbed by the unaccustomed load. All that is required is for the rider to sit perfectly still, refraining from all influencing movements, and to drive the horse well forward into a quiet trot by means of the whip. All tensions in his muscles and his mechanism, resulting from the disturbance of his equilibrium and from his fear, will thus best be removed.

It is of great advantage if the young horse can be ridden alongside an old leading horse, as he will soon imitate the quietness of the older animal.

For the first few lessons one must move on immediately after mounting, because the rider's weight will be felt more disagreeably at the halt than at the forward movement, when the tension in the muscles soon disappears.

As soon as the horse has become used to the rider's weight, he will again show his natural paces, which until then will have been somewhat insecure, shorter and hastier. Quiet, regular, long strides are a sign that the first goal has been reached. Influences of the hand could only hinder the attainment of this goal. One should be careful not to tire the youngster, nor to overwork him, by too long a trot or by extending the lessons too long. As soon as a horse feels any kind of a pain he gets excited.

Quiet walks in between trots, stroking and patting the neck, and talking in a low and quiet voice will do a lot more in these walk intervals than all 'aids'. The greatest help, however, is a quiet seat ! It is wrong to assume that the rider can relieve the horse's hind quarters by giving up the base of his seat and leaning forward. At the slightest start of the horse he will topple forward and thus disturb the horse more than if he had followed all the latter's movements with a supple but braced back. It is quite impossible for a rider to make things more comfortable for the horse than by being *supple*. By leaning backward he would be heavy and rigid in the saddle; he could not possibly acquire the feeling for following the movements of the horse. Such a rider should never attempt to break a young horse !

SECOND STAGE OF SCHOOLING

'PUTTING THE HORSE TO THE AIDS'

This stage is so important for the whole of the dressage system and is so frequently misunderstood that it must be discussed very thoroughly. This will be done according to the following schedule:

(a) What is meant by 'putting the horse to the aids' ?

(b) What does a horse look like when 'put to the aids' ?

(c) How is a horse 'put to the aids' ?

(d) What mistakes, doubt and questions thereby arise ?

(e) Can the rider himself discover whether his horse has been properly 'put to the aids' ?

What is meant by 'putting the horse to the aids' ?

A horse is properly 'put to the aids', or 'stands at the aids' if the following has been attained:

(1) That the horse is fully relaxed. There must be no tenseness or rigidity of any kind, either in the jaws, in the poll, the neck, the back or the legs, nor in any joint or muscle—nowhere.

(2) That the horse is properly 'between the legs', 'at the rider's back', 'at the reins' and 'in equilibrium'. That means that the whole of the moving mechanism of the horse must be willingly put at the disposal of the rider. This naturally comprises also that the horse understands the influences of legs, hands, weight and back and that it

5

is prepared and ready willingly to obey those indications. Being 'put to the aids' does *not*, however, mean:

(1) a certain position or carriage of the horse, or

(2) that the horse can already understand and obey the 'aids' which are composed of the various influences.

At this stage the relaxed horse should willingly and with full confidence carry out the simplest things which the rider asks of him. This, at the trot and at the canter, should give the rider a feeling of harmony and co-ordination; at the walk and at a standstill the feeling will come much later. Thus the basis is created on which to continue the education. Without the horse's goodwill and his confidence in the rider, and without his being fully relaxed, co-operation and harmony between them is hardly conceivable. Even if only one of the above described conditions is not truly fulfilled, there will always be difficulties of some sort, which may in turn lead to a catastrophe, or will at least bring about circumstances under which the rider will not be able to carry out his intentions. All this depends on the character of the horse and the horsemanship of the rider.

To 'put the horse to the aids' is therefore the fundamental basis, the starting-point for all dressage. Also it is the best preparation for all and any purposes for which the rider intends later on to use his mount (such as jumping). In the course of the training each and every lesson should be started by 'putting the horse to the aids', be the lesson an easy or a difficult one. The rider must first secure attention, looseness and willingness from his horse and can only then expect that the animal will submit to his will.

'Putting the horse to the aids' is also the starting-point to which the rider must return if his horse shows the slightest indication of disobedience, bad habits, tenseness or difficulties of any kind. Ruined or badly mouthed horses, which have lost their natural 'go' or have become timid and shy, must first of all be 'put to the aids' again. As soon as this has been accomplished all difficulties, tensions and so on will disappear, the natural movements will return, and in short, the harmony between rider and horse will be re-established.

The maintenance of this harmony and its perfection in the execution of all, even the most difficult lessons, must in future be the criterion and indicate whether the dressage is proceeding on the proper lines. Each little bit that is added to the edifice of dressage serves to perfect this harmony; if it does not, it must inevitably lead in the wrong direction. That sounds very simple, yet it is well-nigh the most difficult thing in the art of riding, and at the same time also the most important, because it is the indispensable basis of all good riding.

It must not be overlooked that few horses have ever been properly (if at all) 'put to the aids', and that most horses can be more or less well managed across country even without perfect harmony. It is quite certain, however, that the same horses if they had been properly 'put to the aids' would move about with much less exertion, that the rider would feel much more comfortable and safer, and that he would assuredly not find himself face to face with unexpected difficulties. *If* the horse had been 'properly put to the aids' !

What does a horse look like when 'put to the aids' ?

This question is posed here merely because riding pupils often think of the matter in that way. It cannot be answered by describing a particular 'bearing or carriage of the horse' recognized as being the best or most desirable. This would lead the majority of riders to lure or force their horses into that posture, a procedure which contains a great danger for every rider ! It leads him to deceive not only others but himself, so that later on he cannot distinguish between right and wrong. 'Carriage' or 'bearing' will always vary, and must correspond to the degree of dressage and to the character and conformation of the horse. The correct answer to the question posed above, therefore, can only be: 'As if there is perfect harmony between rider and horse'.

This means that the 'carriage' of the horse—if one wished to refer to it at all—must not be described alone, but that the expression 'being put to the aids' includes also the rider, without whom the phrase has no meaning.

Unfortunately, as a rule, descriptions of 'correct positions' do not even cover the whole horse, but refer only to the position of his neck and head. Such descriptions are dangerous because the rider should never forget—and it cannot be said often enough—that he has a living being under him who must be thought of on every occasion *as a whole*. One cannot work single members, apart from the rest of the horse's anatomy, and one must not, either, judge the whole horse by judging parts of him.

The statement that harmony between man and mount should be visible, indicates that a single brief glance does not suffice really to recognize it. It is necessary to observe both the horse and the rider for some time before it is possible to say whether the horse has been 'put to the aids' or not. And it is necessary to observe them at the halt as well as in motion, at changing the lead at the canter, going through corners, in parades, on circles and so forth.

For it is quite possible that a horse may be neatly put 'to the aids' at the trot but not at the halt. If the case appears to be the other way round, however, the horse *seeming* to be 'at the aids' during the halt but not when in motion, then our eyes have most certainly deceived us. Even experienced riders will now and again fall victims to deceptions of this kind, because man in general is prone to draw conclusions on the whole from superficial details. The keener one's knowledge of a certain thing the more difficult it is to avoid over-valuation of certain details to which one attaches special importance.

Every movement must be quiet and harmonious and must

look it. Not only must the whole carriage be harmonious, but every single movement of the horse as well as the rider must be harmonious in itself and in collaboration with the rest. The horse must give us the impression that he feels comfortable, and the rider must look as if he were doing nothing at all but that everything were, so to speak, going by itself. This latter request, i.e. that the aids should be invisible,

In order to emphasize the danger which lies in the over-estimation of external appearance, no illustration of a horse put to the aids is given.

HARMONY between
RIDER AND HORSE

should exist not only at a particular favourable moment, such as might be caught by a photograph. It is not manifested in a special carriage, but in the lasting unity of both bodies in every movement.

Fig. 19. THE HORSE PUT TO THE AIDS

is of the utmost importance. Whenever the aids can be *seen* they are not harmonious, and it can be concluded with certainty that the horse has never been properly 'put to the aids'.

(1) The RIDER[1] must:

(a) sit steadily, quiet and supple at the lowest part of the saddle. One must neither see nor hear his buttocks plop into the saddle at every stride.

[1] Judicial observation of man and mount can be started at the rider or at the horse. We shall here start with the rider, because he is the active part.

(b) keep his arms and hands completely quiet. He must not beat time with his hands nor must the lower arms swing about. The reins must be continuously taut, and not hang loosely for part of the time and then be drawn taut again. Contact with the horse's mouth must not be sought by jerking or see-sawing with the reins.

(c) keep his legs quietly and continuously in contact with the horse's body so that they can act at any moment without any alteration of their position being necessary. Only the knee will move, and that hardly perceptibly: it will have to be bent a little more.

(2) The horse must:

(a) show quiet, regular, but lively steps.

(b) be perfectly straight in the forward movement, with both ears at the same height; in corners and turns, he must flex towards the inside. The slightest glance to the outside betrays stiffness.

(c) chew quietly and steadily at the bit, without being heard. He must not try to push the bit forward, nor gnash or crunch it; nor must he play with his tongue, get it over the bit, or let it hang out of his mouth or develop too much foam.

(d) carry his neck and head quietly. He must not shake his head, not even when trotting on from a halt, or when changing gaits or halting. He must not stretch his neck or rest his head on the chest, and must not from time to time snap back towards his chest. The neck must show a nicely rounded line, without a break in it.

(e) carry his tail quietly without swishing or twisting it.

All the above conditions must prevail simultaneously. Should one of them be missing it would be impossible for the horse to be really relaxed and supple and to put his full mechanism at the disposal of the rider. He would not be properly 'put to the aids'.

The rounding of the neck and the chewing at the bit are *neither the only nor the most important features*; they are only the easiest to recognize. There are, however, many ways of making a horse round his neck or chew the bit (in order superficially to meet the requirements) without his being really and honestly 'put to the aids'.

HOW IS A HORSE 'PUT TO THE AIDS'?

This question must be answered in various ways according to whether it concerns:

(1) a green horse.

(2) a well-made horse.

(3) a badly-made horse.

Ways and means in each of these cases are fundamentally the same. But in order to make the matter quite clear we will discuss them separately.

That which can be achieved on a well-made horse by simple aids requires weeks of carefully planned work with a green horse, and thorough corrections with a badly or poorly made horse that opposes the rider's will. 'Putting a horse to the aids' has therefore been described as a 'stage'. If a horse passes the tests for being put to the aids, he has successfully passed this stage.

The 'putting to the aids' of a well-made horse. If a rider wants to put a schooled horse to the aids all he has to do is to brace his back. Whether at the halt, or at the walk, the trot, or the canter—the horse will immediately be at the aids, provided that there is a 'sustaining' effect on the reins, i.e. that they be completely passive, and provided that the rider's legs, which must always have contact with the horse's body, support the

action of the back or loins by a slight additional pressure.
(See half-halt, p. 113.)

The main impulse must therefore come from the rider's
back and legs, and not from the reins.   It is wrong to shorten
the reins by screwing-in the fists.

A horse that is not immediately put to the aids by a bracing
of the back and a slight leg pressure is not properly schooled.
It is either a green horse or a badly made one.

Putting a green horse to the aids.   A raw horse can be 'put to the
aids' as soon as he can comfortably carry the rider's weight at a
quiet working trot, going forward with long, easy strides at
the side of a leading horse.   Proper work starts as soon as the
horse begins to get, as it were, lazy, the rider being forced to
urge him on.   The preliminaries preparatory to making the
horse understand this urging on are done with the whip.
In using the whip, however, the rider must proceed very
cautiously, especially with a youngster, lest he frighten or
startle him.   With his lower legs the rider must then 'feel'
himself closer and closer to the horse's body; no horse will
resent this, provided the legs remain steady and quiet.   A light
tap with the whip given simultaneously will make the horse
understand that 'leg pressure' means 'urging on'.

From then on, all further work consists in riding the horse
well forward at a quiet working trot.   The pace should be
just a trifle faster than the one the horse offers voluntarily to
go.   As soon as he shows an inclination to get shorter and
slacker in his stride, the swing and liveliness of the pace will
be lost.   By urging him on and forward the rider begins to
impose his will upon the horse; it must be the rider who deter-
mines the pace and not the horse.   This is the beginning of all
'putting to the aids'.   The free forward movement must not
be impaired by the rider's hands trying to 'shape' the horse at
the same time, because 'shape' or 'form' are not what counts
here.   All tensions and all one-sidedness which become

apparent, as well as all short or nappy strides must, so to say, be ridden out forward, in a quiet, striding trot. The horse will thereby quite naturally drop his head and neck—provided the rider does not work against it with his hands—and he will on his own initiative try to find a steady support on the bit.

Great care should be taken not to change the pace too early or too suddenly; i.e. not to attempt the middle trot. Changes of direction and pace must be only slightly indicated, as an experiment, as it were. It must all be done step by step, and it is most important never to lose the quiet, regular forward stride. When a free forward movement can be maintained it is time to ask a little more of the horse, but immediately the free swing of the movement is lost we must realize that we have asked too much of him.

Thus one little success will come after another, each resulting from a previous one. After a short time the horse will readily obey the urging legs. As a result of his hind quarters being constantly driven forward by the legs he will accept the bit and begin to chew it. That is what makes it so important that the rider's hands should remain completely passive: the horse must find the bit himself. The rider must never attempt to expedite this by pulling on the reins! This would involve a grave danger of the horse's head coming behind the vertical line and of his beginning to play with the bit.

The horse must never be 'behind the bit' or try to spit it out. This can only be prevented by increased urging on and by freer and longer strides. If this is of no avail a light tap with the whip will do the trick. If the rider hears the horse playing with the bit, trying to spit it out, he should again give him a light tap with the whip and drive him well forward. The quiet, regular working pace must be more and more confirmed. Firmness and steadiness of the forward stride are the best testimony to the correctness of the rider's system of training his mount. If, with his supple and quiet seat, he gradually increases the action of his back during the halts and if all changes of direction and all turns are harmoniously supported by correct shifting of the weight, the young horse will, after some time, firmly and securely 'be at the aids'.

A firm seat, glued to the saddle as it were, and gradually increased actions of back and legs will bring the horse quite automatically into the passive hands. A forcing of head and neck into position by pulling at the reins, be it done ever so cleverly, must needs lead to wrong results. The animal, thanks to its rounded neck, may perhaps thus give the impression of a perfectly made horse; but he has by no means really become obedient. But he has, on the other hand, acquired the art of evading the rider's influences by curling the neck and 'creeping behind the bit'.

Putting a badly-made or a ruined horse to the aids. A ruined or badly-made horse is one that has carried a rider for some time without being properly at the aids, and one that at the same time cannot be properly put to the aids merely by the rider bracing his back, as would be the case with a well-made and well-schooled horse.

There is no denying that any rider will make a better figure on a well-made horse than on a badly-made one. Further, it is very instructive and even necessary from time to time to try out the efficiency of one's influences on well-made and sensitive horses. It would, however, be absolutely wrong to conclude that one can only learn to ride on a perfectly-made horse. 'Feel' is acquired by comparison; by riding many horses that give one different and varied 'feels'. A rider who has never had an opportunity of learning how it feels when a horse is 'behind the bit' cannot yet have a definite and well-developed feel for the horse 'being at the aids'. A well-made and sensitive horse can soon be ruined by wrong influences and by wrong aids and can also quickly be brought 'behind the bit'. And if one does not know how to put a horse to the

aids there is always the danger of unconsciously and involuntarily bringing the horse 'behind the bit'. Such a rider
must needs mistrust his feel and his influences. It therefore
belongs to the complete education of a rider that he occupy
himself with the following.

The young rider, however, should not start too early with
his attempts to re-school a ruined horse, unless he has really
learned to follow the movements—stick to the saddle—in his
riding.

Horses which cannot be put to the aids by a mere bracing
of the back evade the rider's influences in various ways and
in various degrees. This bad habit may be very deeply rooted,
but it may also be superficial. Sometimes it suffices to ride the
horse strongly forward into the passive hand. (See also p. 106.)

The more a certain disobedience has become a regular habit,
the more carefully must the rider plan how to proceed in
order to 'drive it out' in the true (riding) sense of the word.

A horse will seldom evade the influences of the rider in one
particular manner only; almost always he will display several
bad habits simultaneously. The only way to correct them all
is by working the whole animal and not the affected parts
only.

The principal bad habits are the following; one says of a
horse that he :

is hard mouthed,
is rigid at the poll,
leans on the bit,
jogs at the walk,
has a wrong bend in the neck (behind the third vertebra),
has short nappy paces (if hot tempered),
goes one-sided,
gets the tongue over the bit,
beats with his head (see martingale, p. 179),
is a star gazer,

is ewe-necked,
goes behind the bit,
gives way in the back (with hot, but weak horses),
is stiff in one or both hind legs,
throws himself against the leg.

All these bad habits disappear immediately the horse is properly 'put to the aids'. In the end they are nothing but symptoms of the same evil, namely, the attempt to 'evade the aids', showing itself in various ways.

The procedure must always be the same, differing only in so far as one or other of the required conditions is easier or more difficult to bring about, or is perhaps already present. For such work it is always of advantage to use a plain snaffle, which all horses are more inclined to accept. The snaffle acts much more softly than the curb, and the horse will more readily take to it.

(1) A horse must first learn to go forward in response to driving or urging influences.

(2) As soon as this is accomplished, he should be flexed towards the inside.

(3) If he can be flexed towards the inside, he must be shown the way to lower his head.

(4) As soon as he has lowered his head, he must be taught to 'find the bit'.

(5) If he accepts the bit, he is being pulled up by half parades.

How is a badly-made horse taught to obey the driving influences ? The greatest difficulty arises with horses who run away because they cannot bear the 'leg'. Some riders believe that such horses must never be urged on at all. In these cases all depends on being able to steady and quieten the animals down. To this end it is necessary to ride at a quiet trot on a circle, and if that does not help, in the 'volte' (small circle). The

HORSE 'OVER THE REINS'
(with stiff neck)

Rider's hands too low, legs stretched away, no co-operation of his influences

Not to be recognized by a picture whether horse :

LEANS ON THE BIT, *if the rider has too much weight in his hands or* **BEHIND THE BIT,** *if he has no weight in them at all, the reins from time to time hanging slack*

EWE-NECK—HOLLOW BACK

Hefty, high steps. Too much erection obtained by influences of hands without sufficient driving influence, no collection, no lowering of hind quarters

Fig. 20. BADLY SCHOOLED HORSES

which are not properly 'at the aids.'

rider, however, must not attempt to pull at the reins; the reins have no other task than to indicate the direction. And one must remain on the circle or in the volte until the horse can be driven forward without storming away. The better one understands the principle of sticking to the saddle and bracing the back, and the more cautiously and quietly the legs keep contact with the horse's body, the quicker will this be accomplished. Every sudden or hasty movement with an unsteady leg will frighten the horse and make him run away again. The continuous short turns of the volte will gradually quieten down any horse. There is no other or better means. The rider will thus be able to begin the urging on very much sooner than he would have thought, but only if he really understands the principle of sticking to the saddle.

This keeping quiet in the saddle (not rigid, not heavy, but supple, with braced loins) is most important, even imperative for success, on horses that suffer with pains in their back. Trying to sit more forward or leaning forward does not lead to the desired result. The inner rein keeps the horse on the circle or in the volte; the outer rein can be neglected for the time being, and the carriage of the horse's head or neck is of no importance at this stage. What is essential is that the rider should determine the pace, and not the horse. Proper schooling can begin only when this has been achieved. Dressage cannot be started unless the horse has become 'lazy' and needs to be driven forward, so that the rider has a chance to exert his influences with his back and legs.

With horses who by nature are lazy and dull the reverse is the case. It would be wrong to confine oneself to driving them forward with the legs alone. And spurs only hurt unnecessarily and make them still more apathetic. The only thing to be done is to apply the whip (see p. 181). Even the green horse will learn to go forward if whip, back and leg influences all act at the same time. The rider must therefore have acquired all necessary knowledge as to the use of the whip before he can attempt to put such a horse to the aids. If a horse has learned to go forward in response to back and leg action, the rider will soon be able to determine the working pace; it must be quiet, regular and steady, but (as has been said before) always just a little faster than the horse wants to go of his own accord. To forget this is the most frequent and most serious mistake made when putting a horse to the aids.

Why and how is a badly-made horse worked 'in position'?
As soon as the spoilt horse has learned to go forward upon back and leg action he must be taught to 'flex'.

In order to be 'put to the aids' the horse must be fully relaxed and the easier one makes it for the animal the sooner it will do what the rider wants.

All horses loosen up quickly if they are flexed. It is a fact that all horses by nature go more or less flexed to one side, either to the left or to the right, but never perfectly straight. Most other quadrupeds are the same, as can be observed with dogs. The effect of flexing is most apparent with horses that have a weak back.

The rider flexes the horse towards the inside by cautiously pulling at the inner rein, at the same time giving slightly with the outer rein. Almost any horse can thus very soon be flexed towards the inside. If it does not go on the right side it will go on the left. It is up to the rider to find out which side suits his horse best. By changing from one hand to the other on the circle or in the volte (correct figures) it is not very difficult to feel this, and it does not require a great deal of horsemanship. Work should begin on the side towards which the horse flexes most willingly. Incidentally, it is of no importance whether the horse is flexed first at the neck and then at the hind quarters or vice versa, as long as it is not forgotten that *riding forward* is and remains the decisive point and that each neglect of the rider's seat must lead to very dubious results.

If a horse, despite decisive urging on and against all expectations, persistently refuses to bend or flex, recourse must be taken to the sliding rein (see p. 180). But there are very few horses who cannot be flexed on at least one side if the rider sits softly but firmly in the saddle and carefully acts with the inner rein.

Use of the sliding rein seems to complicate things a little, but in certain cases it is unavoidable. It is, however, imperative that the rider be fully conversant with its use before starting to work with it, and as soon as it has fulfilled its purpose it must be discarded—otherwise the damage will be greater than the gain. The more softly the inner rein is employed the quicker will the horse flex towards the inside providing that at the same time the outer rein 'gives' and the horse is energetically driven forward. If the rider uses crude force with the inner rein he must not be surprised if the horse, being a great deal stronger than he, does not answer immediately by softly giving in. The decisive factor for success will be the degree of caution used in treating the horse's mouth at the beginning. All the time the horse must, of course, be strongly ridden forward with a well-defined shifting of the weight. If one is not lucky on one hand one should try the other, and if the horse does not go on the circle, try him in the volte. Changing from the left to the right hand and from the right to the left hand also helps, but the difficulties must not be increased by hanging on to the outer rein.

As soon as flexion is obtained the inner rein has only one task and that is: to secure that the flexion is not lost. If it is —if only for the fraction of a second—the work must be interrupted and suppleness, i.e. flexion towards the inside, re-established immediately.

Why and how should a badly-made horse be 'shown the way to the ground'? To many riders it is not at all clear why it should be necessary first to obtain a low position of the horse's head and

neck when the ultimate end
of his future education is to
raise his forehand and lower
his hind quarters. Raising the
forehand has no value and is
of no use at all unless it is the
consequence of the lowering
of the hind quarters (relative
erection). The hind quarters
must show more acute angles
and must be lowered in order
to take a bigger share in
carrying the load (see p. 99).
To this end they must be
properly trained. First of all
the hind legs must be made
to step well forward; this
develops and strengthens the
respective muscles. As soon
as a horse pushes his hind-
hand forward he naturally
lowers his neck (see p. 97).

But the neck should not
only be lowered, it should
also be *stretched*, and the
stretching is perhaps even
more important than lowering. If one cannot make a
horse stretch his neck, one has
no chance of preventing his

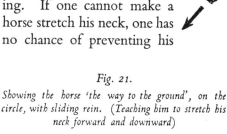

Fig. 21.
Showing the horse 'the way to the ground', on the
circle, with sliding rein. (Teaching him to stretch his
neck forward and downward)

6

creeping behind the bit and thus evading the influences of the reins. Hence one is never in a position really to 'put the horse to the aids'.

This lowering and stretching of the horse's neck is called 'showing the horse the way to the ground'. The work is best started on the circle or in the volte at a quiet working trot. At first the rider exerts a very slight pressure upon the outer jaw so that he can immediately 'give' by slightly bringing his fist or the whole arm forward towards the horse's mouth. This slight pressure must only last a second and has no other purpose than to draw the horse's attention to the outer rein: the important thing is the 'giving'. By this 'feeling forward' of the reins the horse, in turn, should be induced to give and stretch his neck. The rider's legs meanwhile are continuously pressing the horse forward, keeping the pace lively and making it just a fraction faster than the horse wants to go. As soon as the rider forgets to urge on, or if the horse begins to determine the pace, there is no longer any reason for him to go up to the bit, and the whole work is useless. This driving forward and urging on must, then, be most determined when the outer hand is giving and 'feeling forward', and the rein, so to speak, acting in a luring or baiting manner.

For this kind of work the rider does not require any particular 'feel', but, on the other hand, his feel is developed by it. The inner hand is only concerned with maintaining flexion and must not attempt to support the activity of the outer hand. This is important because otherwise the rider is tempted to act with both hands alternately; he would begin to work to and fro with his hands, or, in other words, see-saw with the reins. In this way a horse can never be 'put to the aids'. He is more likely to be brought 'behind the bit' or taught to lean heavily on it.

If the rider can induce the horse to stretch his neck by continuously giving with the outer hand, that is, if he makes him stretch up to the bit, the horse will gradually comply with his wish. There will be no painful sensation; the horse is more likely to find it boring and more or less insignificant, and will not oppose it for that reason, but will gradually become duller and lazier the longer he is kept on the circle or in the volte. Provided the rider does not get impatient the horse will gradually stretch himself on to the bit. If the rider finds that this takes too long he can try to flex the horse a bit more. Or he can attempt to urge a little more so that he presses him on to the outer rein. He can also try to discover whether the horse understands quicker on the other side. But more than this the rider cannot and must not do. He can only show his horse 'the way to the ground'; the animal must find it for himself.

Most horses will react after a few minutes; hard-boiled sinners may take half an hour, but sooner or later any horse will respond to this 'feeling forward' and to constantly being 'offered' the bit. As soon as the horse has made his first timid attempt to stretch his neck, the rider should do nothing but continue to urge him well forward with legs and back and on to the outer rein; first on one hand, then on the other hand and a little more intensely on the horse's softer side, so that some definite progress can at last be seen and so that the horse can understand that he has done what was asked of him. The same thing is then repeated on the other hand. The rider must continuously change the hand (correct track figures) until the horse stretches his neck equally well on both sides, *forward* and *downward*. At this moment the basis for 'putting him to the aids' is created.

How does the badly-made horse 'find the bit'? As soon as the horse comfortably stretches his neck all the rider has to do is to utilize this forward urge and to let the reins act passively. The horse will then quite automatically lean on the bit and begin to chew it. If he is not being forced in any way, beyond being energetically ridden forward, there is no cause for stiffness, rigidity, tenseness or fear. Therefore the stretching of the neck is the first requirement, the *conditio sine qua non*, for enabling the horse to find and accept the bit. The stretching of the neck, however, is just as little identical with 'accepting the bit' as formerly the obtaining of flexion was with the stretching of the neck. All three actions,

> flexing,
> stretching of the neck,
> obtaining contact with the bit,

are more or less merged into one another; much more so than may perhaps appear from this description, but it is necessary to describe them separately in order to explain them properly.

The most important thing always remains the driving forward, and it must never be forgotten that the horse must again and again be driven up to the bit. The outer hand must always ascertain whether the contact between the hand and the horse's mouth is really a consequence of this driving forward and not the result of a pull at the reins !

All rigidities and stiffness in the jaws, poll, neck, back, and legs must disappear as a consequence of a boringly even and regular, yet energetic pace, always a little faster than the horse wants to go. The horse will relax more and more, and in the end will go well balanced, being at the disposal of the rider's legs, back and reins.

When the horse willingly accepts the bit he is taken up by half-halts. By means of the above exercises the horse will have been 'put to the aids'. All that is now required is to stabilize and confirm what has been achieved. The horse must again and again be caused to stretch his neck so that this way of going, which he cannot but find comfortable, is firmly established. The strides will become more and more quiet and, through constant driving and urging, longer. The horse's back will begin to swing pleasantly, it will be rounded with each step, and all muscles will play freely. If the reins are then slightly 'sustained' the horse will not only chew the bit if he is driven up to it, but will yield to the pressure of it. He will, without resistance, allow himself to be 'taken up', i.e. to transfer more weight to his hind quarters, and to halt. This kind of work gradually leads to the teaching of 'collection' (see p. 96).

The above procedure will not produce the desired result in half an hour, and not with each and every horse. Sometimes it will take the rider eight to fourteen days to confirm and establish these lessons, so that he can put his mount to the aids after a few steps, like a perfectly made horse. But if the movement does

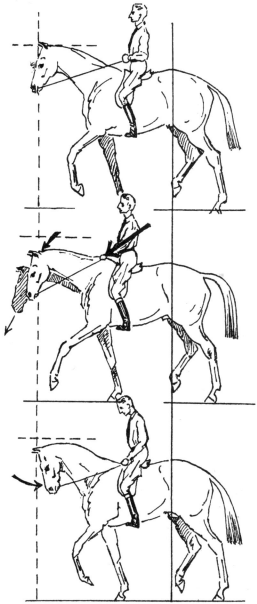

Fig. 22. LENGTHENING THE STRIDE
as opposed to wrong 'bridling'

not come within this number of lessons, it will most probably never come at all, for it will never come by itself or by mere chance. In this event the rider should ask himself if the reason for his failure does not perhaps lie in himself. One of the chief reasons for failures is that the rider has not properly learned to follow the horse's movements.

WHAT QUESTIONS, DOUBTS, AND MISTAKES APPEAR DURING THIS WORK ?

The procedure for re-shaping a badly-made horse may appear rather simple in theory. As a matter of fact it is much simpler in practice than is generally assumed. It should be known to every rider because it helps to develop his feel. Any one who has attempted to put a badly-made horse to the aids should be fully aware of the fact that the essential basis for success is positive harmony, that is to say, following the movements of the horse and 'being glued to the saddle'. The rider who has not understood this principle will never be in a position properly to put his horse to the aids, because he cannot adequately influence the horse if he does not fully master the application of the influences.

'Bracing the back' is to some riders utterly incomprehensible. Some talk of their backs and do not begin to know what to do with it. Others deny altogether the possibility of exerting any influence with it. Many do not believe in its use because they have never experienced what it means to 'push' the horse's mouth forward (as if the reins were rigid rods) and to extend his neck; or again, they think that these requirements are so difficult to comply with that only a few gifted artists can do them justice. Such riders sometimes do not even dare to give a horse the reins lest he extend his head and they find themselves unable to round his neck again and thus completely lose control over him. In consequence such riders try to 'bridle' their horses by pulling at the reins. Unfortunately the expression 'bridling' gives the impression that this is the correct way of doing it (see p. 100). If the horse resents it (and quite justly, too) the rider pulls a little more or begins to see-saw with his hands; and if then the horse suddenly yields, the reins fall slack for the fraction of a second and the rider, frightfully pleased, thinks he has achieved something big and makes much of his horse. No longer feeling weight in his hands, he forgets to drive the horse forward and into the bridle—and, lo and behold, the first step has been taken towards getting the horse to 'be behind the bit' ! Horses very quickly learn to evade the pressure of the bit by snapping back and rounding the neck, and thus the rider quite unconsciously and involuntarily, but cleverly, *teaches* his horse this bad habit. This unhappy procedure takes place a thousand times a day, and it leads to the famous 'wrong bend' in the neck instead of at the poll, just as much as it leads to being behind the bit. This wrong bend in the neck can easily be detected and looks rather ugly.

Riders are often recommended to put a horse to the aids first at the halt or at the walk, and then at the trot. This is wrong because it is much more difficult than the other way round. The rider wants a lot more feel and experience for it. The forward movement of the trot makes most riders realize much more intimately that they must not confine their activities to the neck and head of the horse, but that the whole animal must be worked. Also it is easier at the trot than at the halt or at the walk to feel whether the horse is responding to the driving influences and whether he is going well forward or not.

'That the rider should give as soon as the horse gives' is advice which is very often misunderstood, and which is the cause of innumerable mistakes. It means only that the rider should never maintain a continuous pull; taking up the reins should not last longer than until the horse has given. If the rider keeps on pulling, in spite of the horse having yielded, it must needs lead to differences between man and mount for which the horse cannot be blamed.

The above cited sentence is very often misinterpreted in another way: 'The rider shall give after the horse has given'. In other words, he shall pull at the reins long enough to make the horse give. Advice given in this form must, of course, lead to mistakes. If the horse does not give as soon as the bit exerts pressure on the jaws the cause will very often be found in the fact that the rider has not at the same time acted energetically enough with his back and with his legs, as he should do, for instance, in halting. In this case a little increased influence will perhaps be sufficient to obtain obedience. If the repetition of the halt in a better 'edition' is not sufficient, in other words, should the horse continue to lean heavily on the bit, then the rider is faced with the task of making his horse give by 'showing him the way to the ground'. If he tries to pull at the reins until the horse has found this way all by himself the 'giving'— provided it ever happened—would not be to the rider's credit, for it would not be the result of his influences, but mere chance and luck. The rider would have done nothing but wait in the hope that the horse would graciously consent to give in. With the majority of riders, however, this procedure results in a tug-of-war. Should the horse by any chance yield in this struggle for the fraction of a second (although he is ten times the stronger) the rider will, in ninety-nine out of a hundred cases, miss the long expected moment and give with the reins too late. And if he is lucky enough to hit on the right moment, the chances are that the horse will get 'behind the bit'. In exceptional cases a very clever rider may perhaps still be able to make the horse understand that he should stretch his neck; but if he succeeds in this piece of art then it is due to a clever 'feeling forward' and not to the pull at the horse's mouth ! The procedure was, no doubt, wrong because the pulling had only increased the difficulty of the job.

CAN THE RIDER DISCOVER FOR HIMSELF WHETHER HIS HORSE
STANDS CORRECTLY AT THE AIDS ?

A special chapter is devoted to this question because
many riders are inclined to deceive themselves. The question
is most important because the success of all further work
depends on it. Empty phrases such as 'one can see that' or 'one
must feel it' are not answers.

If a horse has been correctly put to the aids it must:

(1) be completely relaxed.
(2) 'stand at legs and back' (obey leg action and bracing
    of back).
(3) 'stand at the bit' (obey the reins), and
(4) be balanced.

Each of these four points will be dealt with separately in
order fully to explain these *termini technici*.

It must not be assumed that these four requirements can be
achieved independently; they merge into one another. All
aids are combinations of back, leg, rein, and weight influences
which cannot be separated from one another. It is impossible
to put a horse to the bit without the legs, nor is it possible to
put him to the legs without the reins. A horse can only be
'put to the aids'.

Thoroughness in these questions is indispensable, and there
must not be the slightest doubt as to what the rider should
actually feel.

How does the rider feel whether his horse is relaxed ? This
question is a very comprehensive one, and the correct answer
will only come as the result of all the various tests and examina-
tions described in the following chapters.

A horse is not completely relaxed if there is the slightest
resistance anywhere in its mechanism. In particular : if the

horse (*a*) does not move on in quiet, regular, long strides, and if he does not chew the bit, (*b*) if his back does not swing softly enough to enable the rider to stick to the saddle without great difficulty.

How does the rider feel whether his horse 'stands at legs and back' ?
The tests as to whether a horse responds to legs and back are so closely related to each other that they can hardly be separated. Influences of the back without a supporting action of the legs are impossible. This action can be so refined that it is sometimes difficult to say whether the legs just keep passive contact with the horse or whether they exert actual pressure. The rider himself, however, must always feel this difference.

A horse can be called 'obedient to back and legs' if by these two influences it can at any time be made to :

(*a*) go a better pace,
(*b*) lengthen his stride,
(*c*) halt. 'Leg obedience', moreover, includes the power to make the horse :
(*d*) side step.

Tests as to (*a*) and (*d*) need no special explanation. (See also p. 32.)

Greater difficulties, however, will be encountered in trying to lengthen the stride. The rider drives the horse forward by back and leg, at the same time giving him the bit, but the strides must not be hurried or excited, and the horse must not give any indication whatever (such as throwing the head about or twisting the tail) of feeling annoyed by these influences. He should merely increase the length of his strides, which must continue to be quiet and regular. The feel for this can only be acquired by trying it out. After some time, two or three of such increased strides will be sufficient to tell the rider if his horse is 'back and leg obedient'. Without a lot of practice it is impossible to feel it, and there will be the constant danger of spoiling the horse's natural movements without even noticing it. (See Fig. 22, p. 85.)

The opposite test, namely, seeing whether the halt 'goes through',[1] is just as difficult and not less important. There are people who say that if a halt 'goes through' the horse should really stand more at the reins than at back and legs. It is just this instance, however, which shows more clearly than anything else that one cannot differentiate between a horse 'being at the reins' or a horse 'being at the back and the legs'. All one can say is that the horse is 'at the aids' or not. If we try to increase the length of the strides we must, by rights, also make the opposite test, namely, the halt and half-halt. After all, back and legs are the active factors not only in increasing the pace but also in halting (see p. 116). If a horse is pressed forward while the reins remain passive or are kept slightly taut he should shorten his stride and should, as a whole, pull himself up. His action must become shorter and higher, but, again, he must not show in any way, by poking his head up or down or by twisting his tail, turning his neck, or opening his mouth, that being 'pulled up' is a nuisance and uncomfortable.

The rider should have a sensation as if the horse's hind quarters had become lower and as if he had increased the strides, although they have in fact become slower. High-spirited horses will sometimes respond to the leg-pressure at the halt by a very slight movement of the tail. But if a horse twists his tail violently or gives other indications of discomfort when being 'pulled up' we say that the 'halt did not go through'.

Half-halts can be executed in various degrees; they can be gentle or rough. The utmost finesse consists in doing nothing

[1] The expression 'going through' means that the halt or parade affects the whole horse from head to tail. On the other hand we say that the halt or parade gets 'stuck' if the horse answers the pressure of the bit by opening the mouth or snapping back with the head, catching this pressure, as it were, before it can effect the movement of his whole mechanism.

but brace the back. If the rider is obliged at the same time to press the horse forward with the legs, it can still be called a gentle halt. But if he has actually to pull at the reins in order to increase his influence, no matter how slight the pull, then the hàlt is rather a crude one ! Sometimes the rider may not be able to tell whether he has only driven the horse up to the passive reins or whether he has actually pulled at them. It is easier to answer this question if the reins are held in one hand.

If a horse properly stands at back and legs he will readily respond to all other, simpler influences. It is possible to bring a horse's hind quarters away from a wall by increased contact of the outer leg and a simultaneous pushing forward of the inner pelvic bone. If the horse throws himself against the outer leg and tries to move his hind quarters in the opposite direction, then of course he is not properly leg-obedient. The rider should be able to obtain 'flexion' by the slightest of leg-pressures, both on the right and left hand. And this is at the same time the best way to test a horse's leg-obedience.

How does the rider feel whether his horse 'stands at the reins' ?
A horse is rein-obedient if he can at all times be caused to :

    (*a*) carry his head higher or lower;
    (*b*) stretch his neck;
    (*c*) assume position right or left;
    (*d*) abandon position;
    (*e*) abandon carriage.

A horse is properly put to the aids if the rider can carry out all these tests with the reins united in one hand. Active support by back and legs is, however, indispensable. For here, again, one cannot test only whether the horse is at the reins, but whether he is properly put to the aids altogether.

    (1) If the hands are carried higher or lower the horse's head can be raised or lowered to a certain extent, and in like manner it is possible to raise or lower one ear

of the horse by raising or lowering one hand. The horse should willingly and immediately react to these movements. If he does not do so he is not properly at the rein. The limits between which such raising or lowering of the head is possible can be felt either by the resistance of the horse or by the slackness of the reins.

If the rider attempts to make his horse assume a position of the neck or the head which belongs to a more advanced stage of training, it will have disastrous consequences. The position of neck and head must come more or less automatically. The position must, when the horse is first put to the aids, be a low one. Gradually it will get higher and higher as a consequence of the lowering of the hind quarters and the corresponding natural erection of the whole forehand (relative erection).

(2) If the rider gives with both reins while maintaining even leg-pressure the horse should stretch the neck forward and downwards (extend his neck towards the ground). If the horse does not extend his neck the reins will become slack and the horse is not properly at the reins, or is 'behind the bit'.

Some riders try to excuse this slackness of the reins with the words: 'He should carry his own head.' Here Right and Wrong are very close together. In advanced training the horse will actually 'carry himself'. It does not require any more special reminders of aids of the rider for the horse to maintain the carriage he has been asked to assume. That does not mean, however, that the rider must not still be in a position to extend the horse's neck, whenever he wants to. (See p. 196.)

(3) If the rider is giving with the rein on one side only, while maintaining the position of his legs, and

without shifting his weight, the horse should extend
the neck on that side and should try to maintain
contact with the rider's hand. This is important,
because whatever flexion is required, it should not be
obtained only by pulling at the inner rein, but also by
giving with the outer rein.

In riding on the circle, the horse should be put into
position (flexion) by the inner rein,
into carriage (erection) by the outer rein.
This is a well-known axiom. It implies that if the
inner rein ceased to act the direction would be lost,
and if the outer rein ceased to influence, carriage
or erection would be lost. This leads to the next
two tests.

(4) On a circle the rider gives with the inner rein without
doing anything with the outer rein. In order to do
this he must either come forward with the inner
hand or let the rein drop. A horse that is well at the
aids will endeavour himself to maintain contact with
the inner rein and will, therefore, stretch his neck on
the inside. If the outer rein does not give he will,
for the time being, find a support on it and consequently will flex towards the outside of the circle, and
provided the rider continues to put his weight on the
inner pelvic bone the horse will remain on the circle
with the head turned towards the outside. As soon
as the rider abandons the inner weight influence the
horse will go straight on in a tangent to the circle.
And if the rider shifts his weight towards the other
side the horse will change over to the opposite circle.

(5) If, on the other hand, the rider gives with the outer
rein without altering the action of the inner rein the
horse will extend his neck on the outside. This is
equivalent to losing head carriage and the horse will
gradually run in a spiral towards the inside of the

circle. These last two tests (4 and 5) are important for every rider because they show him where there is a weakness, which side is the more supple, and which side can still be improved.

(6) If both reins are taken in one hand, contact with the horse's mouth must still be maintained. The horse must continue to chew. It should not be forgotten that the contact between the rider's hands and the horse's mouth should only be the result of the driving influences of back and legs and not the result of powerful or see-sawing actions of the hands ! *For this reason the rider should be able to carry out any of these tests with all reins in one hand.*

How does the rider feel whether his horse is balanced ? The question has been put in this way because it occurs to most people in this form. All quadrupeds are nearly always balanced (see p. 33). A foal can stand up and run very soon after it has been born, and although it is at first a little shaky and clumsy it is far ahead of the human child, which has to learn to 'balance' on its two legs. Therefore, the young horse very quickly learns how to deal with a rider's weight. That, however, does not mean that the rider's line of gravity coincides with that of the horse (see p. 33 and further). Not until complete co-ordination between the two centres of gravity has been obtained are rider and horse in equilibrium. And it is then that we can say that 'the horse is balanced'. Otherwise the horse will very soon lose his stride, because his mechanism is interfered with. Unfortunately, this is not always noticed at once, and mostly too late.

A 'balanced' horse reacts immediately upon every displacement of the rider's weight. Displacements of the weight forward or backward are difficult to execute without altering or changing the seat. Also they impair the smooth, close contact between rider and horse. As soon, however, as the horse reacts to the 'bracing of the back' it can be said to be balanced. (See p. 90.)

The horse must immediately respond to lateral displacements of the rider's weight, and, according to the influences of back, legs and reins, must either flex or turn. The rider must be able to ride a serpentine track by mere displacements of his weight and without any rein action at all. It follows, of course, that he must drive his horse well forward with back and legs.

When is the horse put straight ? By nature all horses are a little one-sided. It is generally assumed that the reason for this is the position of the embryo while the mare is in foal. Just as most people are right-handed, so most horses are bent a little towards the left. Later on, by the influences of their riders, many horses become better developed on the right hand or off side. Every effort should be made, however, to ride the horse perfectly straight, or, as we say, to 'put him straight'.

A horse which properly stands at the rider's legs and back and goes well up to his bridle is as straight as possible. If he does not go straight to the front he has probably not been quite properly put to the aids. In a freshly raked riding school the hoof-prints show up clearly and the rider can then see whether his feel has deceived him. If the horse is straight the hind legs follow the tracks of the fore legs; if the horse is one-sided, the hoof-prints of the hind legs are to the right or to the left of those of the fore legs.

THIRD STAGE OF SCHOOLING

COLLECTION AND ERECTION

Dressage proper does not begin until the horse, by having been 'put to the aids', is prepared to *obey* these aids. It is beyond the scope of this book to describe the training in all its details, but as far as its general conception and purpose are concerned it should be known to every rider. A clear conception of the final end of dressage is necessary; otherwise one cannot distinguish between right and wrong procedures.

The purpose of 'dressage' is education to absolute obedience, increased efficiency and handiness. The road is a long one, but through various 'lessons' it leads to the most perfect harmony between rider and horse in 'Haute École'. The improvement of suppleness and 'swing' must always be the criterion as to the correctness of the procedure.

The more handiness the rider demands of his horse, and the more frequent and the shorter the various turns to be executed in full harmony, the more importance must be attached to the complete control of the horse's hind quarters, which are his principal source of power.

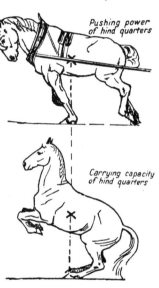

The horse's centre of gravity is nearer to the forehand than to the hind quarters, owing to the fact that the weight of the neck and head rests on the fore legs (see p. 34). The front legs therefore support the greater part of the weight, but the hind legs provide the motive power. Racehorses and steeplechasers carry the bulk of the load on their front legs, as do carriage horses, especially the heavy draught horse.

Fig. 23. TWO EXTREMES

The whole weight either on forehand or hind quarters

This can be nicely observed with horses pulling a heavy van or plough.

The school horse, however, especially if he is to do high-school work, must use his hind legs, not so much for propulsion as for carrying purposes, and they must therefore be made

7

to step well forward and under the centre of gravity. This is called 'collecting', or 'collecting on the hind quarters'. The principle of 'collection' can be studied in the drawings in Fig. 24 where we see that the hind legs, in consideration of the increased demands, are placed more and more forward, under the centre of gravity, until, in the 'Levade' or 'Pesade', they are finally able to carry the whole load alone.

'Collection' is obtained partly by special exercises serving this particular purpose, such as bending the hocks (see Fig. 24), 'side-stepping' and 'shoulder in', and partly by the whole of the training through which the horse is put, as well as by every single 'half-halt'.

Through this kind of work the horse will almost automatically, we might say, contract more and more from rear to front. The hind quarters become lower, the hind legs are busier and more energetic, stepping well forward under the centre of gravity. Not only is the horse more attentive and more prepared to make his best efforts upon the slightest indication of the rider, but he also looks more pleasant and makes a proud impression. For this reason artists of all times have chosen to portray horses in this position when they wished to create an effect of majesty. One thinks of such immortal monuments as the Parthenon frieze and the Pergamon altar of ancient Greece, or the wonderful monument of Prince Eugene in front of the Imperial Palace at Vienna. Velasquez, the great Spanish painter, and David, Napoleon's French portraitist, invariably represented horses in the 'Levade'.

As a consequence of the lowering of the hind quarters the relieved forehand is automatically raised or 'erected'. The front legs show a higher or 'prouder' action, and at the same time the stride becomes shorter (relative erection). This (relative) erection can be increased through active influences by raising the neck and head a little higher, thus shifting the centre of gravity more towards the hind legs, while at the same time energetically driving forward with back and legs (direct

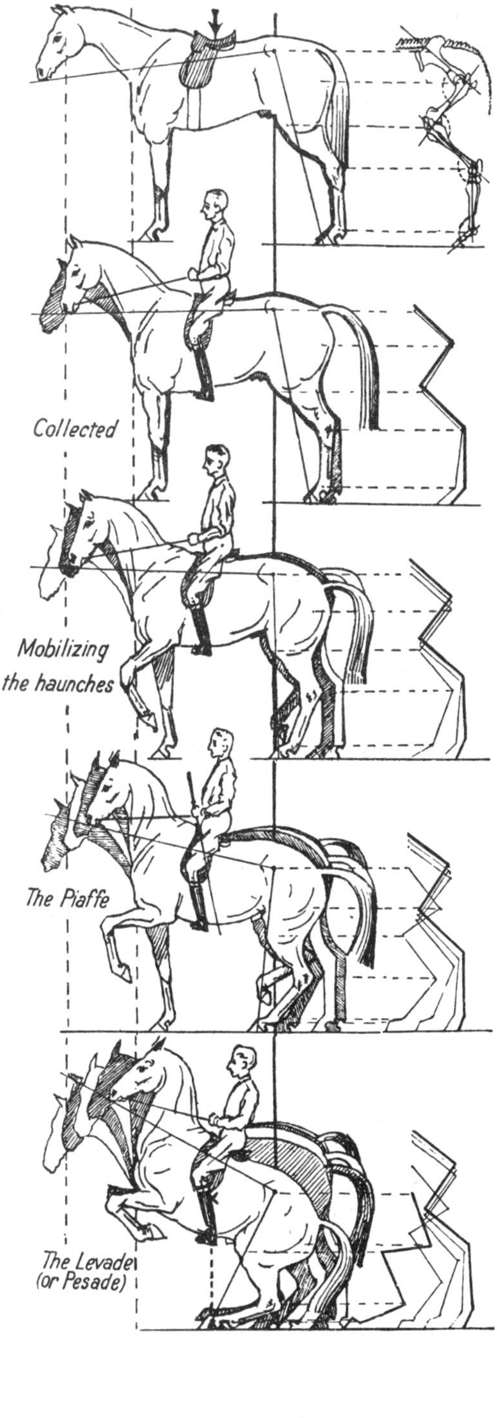

Fig. 24. THE PRIN-
CIPLE OF
COLLECTION
AND ERECTION

*The diagrammatical lines
behind the horses show the
increased angularity of the
haunches and lowering of
the hind quarters*

Collected

Mobilizing
the haunches

The Piaffe

The Levade
(or Pesade)

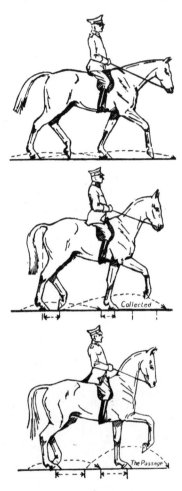

Fig. 25. INCREASED COLLEC-
TION AT THE TROT

*Here we compare three trot movements
which are most typical for the various
degrees of 'collection'—although they
do not represent the same phase of the
trot movement*

erection). It is important, however, that the driving influences
predominate, otherwise the
natural consequence of such
'erection' is a hollow back in the
horse (see Fig. 20)!

'Bridling' means an increased
bend (direct flexion) of poll and
neck. It comes automatically
when the horse is gradually
'collected' by half-halts. This
'bridling' must therefore *not* be
valued as a lesson in itself. If the
rider tries to obtain it by positive
action (mainly pulling at the
reins) it will only result in the
horse either leaning on the bit
or getting behind the bit, or it
would produce the famous 'false
bend' behind the third neck
vertebra.

For this 'collecting' and 'erecting' it is just as important as in
'putting the horse to the aids',
that one should not make the
deplorable mistake of trying to
imitate the picture of a 'collected
horse'. The temptation is strong,
especially if certain single points
are over-valued. 'Collecting'
and 'erecting' a horse must needs
take a long time, unless one does
not mind running the risk of im-
pairing the horse's health. Normally, it should take from one to

two years or even longer, according to the degree of dressage required.

The hind quarters (haunches) must first of all be physically trained and strengthened to make them fit to carry the load. If this process is hurried the horse will probably feel pains; soreness, stiffness, even lameness may result, which, under certain circumstances, may make the horse useless for all future purposes.

All that has been said on p. 70 about a horse being correctly 'put to the aids' applies—and in an increased measure—to the collected horse. Moreover, the collected horse makes a much more energetic and obedient impression. It goes through the most difficult lessons with liveliness and in full swing, yet quiet, and in complete harmony with the rider. And no aids whatever are perceptible.

It is hardly possible to judge the collection of a horse by the carriage of his head and neck alone or by the lowering of his hind quarters. Collection can only be observed by watching him closely during action. As can be seen in the drawings on p. 99, the lowering of the hind quarters at the halt is infinitesimal, and at the walk, even at the passage, it is hardly noticeable. (See sketches on preceding page.)

At the walk a good horse should place his hind hoofs about eight inches ahead of the hoof-prints of his front feet. That can easily be observed when leading a horse (see Plate 2) or when watching him in the paddock, for this is the normal action of an uncollected horse. With increased collection, that is, as soon as the action gets higher as a result of the eased forehand, the action becomes shorter and the hind legs are no longer placed in front of the fore legs. This is shown in the sketches on the preceding page. On the other hand, *this lagging behind of the hind legs is not yet the proof of good collection.* Horses with a lazy action, 'bad movers', tired and overworked horses also leave their hind legs behind. *Another reason not to judge the whole horse by mere details!*

At smarter paces, as at the middle trot or the extended trot, it often happens that a horse 'strikes' his front hoof with his hind hoof. This occurrence, as also a wide straddling step of the hind legs, is an indication that the horse is being asked to go at a better pace than his training allows.

Fig. 26. RIDING IN COLLEC-
TION

At the halt, trot and canter

WHAT IS MEANT BY 'RIDING IN COLLECTION'?

The *terminus technicus* to 'ride a horse in collection' is very often used, but it has purposely been avoided in this book. This expression easily leads to the belief that the 'shape' in which the horse presents itself is the most important thing and that there really exists such a thing as a 'correct position'. And this is supported by the fact that the expression 'bridling' conveys the idea that such a 'correct position' would be looked for in the first place in the pose of head and neck. (For 'bridling', see p. 100.) It has been pointed out repeatedly that all aids should speak always to the whole of the horse, and not to parts only of his anatomy, if the ideal is to be reached, namely, the art of controlling the horse with the minimum of exertion and the maximum of comfort. This principle, which is universally recognized in theory, is very often departed from in practice. There is a belief, even amongst experts, that the procedure which leads to it can be shortened in one way or another. There is also a belief that certain stiffnesses or tensions can be eliminated by special training of the affected parts. The mouth, for instance, is worked by making the horse chew the bit; poll and jaws are worked by 'flexing' or 'breaking' them; and some riders even believe that they can exercise separately any one of the horse's four legs. All these procedures easily lead to complete departure from the cardinal principle. But how can a building be safely erected if we carelessly leave out a bit here and a bit there from the foundation?

Typical expressions for the most frequent errors are 'to shape the horse' and 'to bridle him'. The originally correct conception of these expressions has in practice assumed other meanings. The horse is merely taught to round his neck. The highest point is no longer at the poll but about three hands further back, and forehead and nose are behind the vertical. This gives the horse quite a pleasant appearance; it cannot be called really good, but it certainly looks better than when the neck and head project upwards somewhere to the front.

A horse thus 'bridled' may perhaps feel quite comfortable; he may also execute his paces quietly, but in all probability his strides will be short, in which case we say that he has 'lost his paces'. Such horses are not at all disagreeable to ride, especially for untrained riders in schools or parks, to both of which the horse is probably used. They do not toss the rider, and it is possible for him to sit quite comfortably on them because their action is not high. (For this very reason school horses for beginners should have side reins.) Also, owing to their training, they are a little hard in the mouth and will allow the rider occasionally to hang on to the reins without taking offence.

The real objection to them is that they cannot be obedient, nor in the long run can their legs be saved, because they can never really be collected. The low position of neck and head does not permit the lowering of the hind quarters, and even if it did, it would result in a rounded back, on the top of which the rider would sit as on an arched bridge. 'Bridling' also prevents a free and deliberate stride. But the most deplorable thing about such horses is that they are not properly 'put to the aids', which, of course, means that they are not obedient and that they badly embarrass the rider as soon as he demands of them something that they are not used to or that they do not want to do.

This can be observed again and again, as, for instance, when a young rider wishes to ride away from other horses. His mount becomes 'sticky', and will perhaps rear and kick; he cannot be turned, creeps behind the bit or leans so heavily on it that the poor rider is absolutely helpless. The horse will then follow his own inclination, running after the other horses, and going almost anywhere but in the direction his master wants him to go. It is at such moments that the rider suddenly realizes how much he would like to 'put his horse to the aids', and seeing that it can't be done, he will blame the good-natured animal and perhaps beat it. The horse does not know, of course, why he is being punished, and much as he would like to, he does not and cannot understand the rider.[1] He has probably never learned to go alone, and has always been patted for running along quietly with all the other horses, nicely rounding his neck. It is utterly senseless to punish such an animal with spurs or, as one very often sees it, by jerking him in the mouth.

This type of 'shaping' or 'bridling' may, therefore, result in great difficulties because the 'outer form' has become an end in itself.

The difference between the correct 'being at the aids' and 'riding in position' or 'bridling' is not always quite as clear as

[1] In a quarrel the more intelligent man is always wrong, or else he would not let it come to a quarrel.

that. Every rider thinks or should think while executing a movement, and somehow or other he should work out a plan. But unfortunately if something seems to be beyond him he usually eliminates it from his course of dressage and, without giving it a second thought, is well satisfied with an apparently good result. If he did this fully conscious of the omission, it would not be so bad, but most riders do it unconsciously.

As a warning we will briefly describe the wrong ways frequently employed to 'shape' or 'bridle' a horse.

The preparation for the wrong procedure varies, according to inclination and temperament of rider, instructor, and horse. Some begin with bridling the horse with side reins in the stall to make him chew the bit, taking fairly long reins at first and shortening them gradually until a certain roundness of the neck has been obtained. Some work the horse on foot or on the lunge, with side reins on. Others believe that they can round his neck from the saddle during the halt, without, of course, using any driving influences. Sometimes bridling or chewing of the bit is brought about by a helper on foot, the rider just sitting in the saddle. Often the rounding of the horse's neck is attempted at the halt or at the walk by means of the sliding reins; then a cautious attempt is made to maintain this position during the trot. The horse, of course, strongly adheres to his habits and more or less willingly maintains this position. The nose is brought down and the mouth becomes numb.

The good-natured animal tries to please the inventive rider who, in the end, is mighty proud of having brought his horse into such a 'nice and pleasant shape'.

Ordinary Working Collection

By this position we understand the degree of collection at which a horse is ridden across country. Any horse can go all his paces with more or less collection. The more he is collected the higher will be the action; it requires more force but the stride becomes shorter. It is therefore usual on extended rides to let the horse go in flat, long strides, thereby making better time and saving the animal's legs. If necessary, the horse can be collected at any moment. Over ground with a lot of holes, across ploughed fields, or in the woods, a horse should always be collected in the same degree as in the school.

Dressage collection or dressage carriage

This position, as compared with the ordinary working position, requires an increased collection without, however, representing a *high degree* of collection and erection. The positions for ordinary work and for dressage are *relative* and involve relative degrees of collection, depending on the conformation of the horse. Since, unfortunately, very few riders are able to judge the degree of collection by the whole horse, by the lowering of the hind quarters and by the horse's action, they generally mean a lesser or greater degree of 'bridling' or 'rounding' of the neck.

Some horses have wonderful necks and backs and are riding horses *par excellence*, being particularly suited for dressage and school work; with these, what we should call an 'ordinary working position', would, with horses with thick, heavily-set necks, be called the 'dressage position'.

The increase of the action which takes place with increased collection is shown in Fig. 26, p. 102.

Self-Carriage (or Self-Collection)

By 'self-carriage' we mean the apparently automatic maintenance of the position which the rider has requested the horse to assume. The expression does not refer in any way to a particular degree of collection or a certain outer form. A horse which is properly put to the aids will, with progressive dressage, very soon arrive at this self-collection; it will get there all the sooner the more subtle the rider's aids and the more subtle his rein influences. The opposite of self-collection is the horse leaning heavily on the bit. Self-collection, however, is, as a matter of fact, only an apparently 'natural carriage', because the horse in self-collection must still be worked by the driving seat of the rider and by his passive hands. This so-called self-collection can exist only if there is complete harmony between man and mount. Horses which are behind the bit also assume a position that could be called a certain self-collection. The dividing line between right and wrong is very difficult to recognize and to feel. As soon as the rider is no longer in a position to *lengthen his horse's neck at will, his mount is behind the bit.*

DISOBEDIENCE

Horses do not always do what their riders want. This is generally called 'disobedience', although in most cases it has little or nothing to do with that. The difficulties which arise can be caused by the fact that the rider is not able to convey his wishes to the horse or by the horse showing fear, fright, or suffering pains.

A horse never does anything out of sheer meanness or ferocity ! Exceptions are so rare that they are hardly worth mentioning.

It is very difficult in every single case to find the cause of such difficulties. Mostly there is not a single one, but several working together. This makes the problem so much the more complicated; but it is imperative to get to the root of the matter if the difficulty is to be overcome.

Disobedience very often shows itself in little happenings to which the rider does not pay enough attention and which, therefore, not only increase in number but also in severeness. It is interesting to note that different horses will show the same bad habits under the same rider. It is, therefore, well for the rider first of all to criticize himself and to correct his seat and aids.

'Leaning on the bit', for instance, is generally the consequence of too heavy a hand. In most cases this can be corrected by the rider bracing his back and sitting well down in the saddle, with increased driving influences, or if necessary, with a slight touch of the spurs. If a horse has got used to 'leaning on the bit', having his head, so to speak, carried by the rider's hand, then short but decisive taps with the whip close behind the girth will help. They have to be repeated immediately if the horse tries again to lean on the bit.

Punishment must be instantaneous, but always be administered once only. The horse will be startled, and will make a few faster steps after which he will try again to lean on the bit. He is punished again and so forth until he breaks himself of the bad habit. The most important thing in this procedure, however, is not the whip, nor the spur, but the *continuous driving influences of back and legs.* The procedure with most other bad habits is similar. But if a rider does not endeavour to improve his seat, his feel, and his aids, he will always find the same bad habits coming out in all his horses.

(1) The most common bad habits or disobedience are mentioned on p. 75. They all have their causes in the horse not having been properly put to the aids, and that is mostly the rider's fault and nothing to do with the horse.

(2) Other bad habits, such as: shying, bucking, rearing, running away, sticking, and pressing towards a wall, appear unexpectedly during work and may perhaps prevent the rider from going on.

The kind of disobedience mentioned under (1) is very often the reason for the difficulties mentioned under (2).

The rider should, therefore, not accept them as having come from the gods, but should seriously endeavour to put his horse to the aids so that the difficulties do not arise at the most awkward moments. The procedure of putting the horse to the aids has been thoroughly discussed in the chapter on p. 65

and elsewhere. If difficulties arise in riding across country, it is mostly impracticable to prevent them. It is then that the rider ruefully, but too late, confesses to himself that he would have done well first of all to learn how to put his horse to the aids.

SHYING

A shying horse always turns his head towards the object of his fright, looking and staring at it. He must be turned the other way, away from the object, and must be driven well forward with the inner leg, past the object he is scared of. The decisive point is to change the horse's position, because then he cannot prop himself against the rider's legs. If one does not succeed in turning the horse away from the object and driving him forward, it is best to dismount and to lead him past. One can often pass frightening objects by hanging on to other horses; in this case the horse's head should be turned away from the object before reaching it.

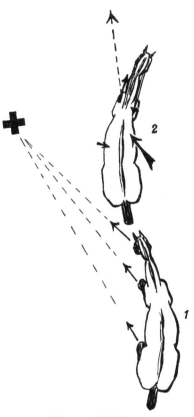

Fig. 27. SHYING

BUCKING

A horse can buck in various ways: plunging forward, on the spot, or on the spot and at the same time swerving. In all three cases he will bring his head down and can quite easily unseat the rider. The rider must, therefore, try to raise head and neck

by strong, lifting jerks at the reins, at the same time driving
forward with determination. If the rider forgets to ride forward in such instances, he will with certainty be 'bucked off',
unless it pleases the horse to stop bucking. Horses with very
tender backs often show an inclination to buck immediately after
having been mounted, especially if they have not been saddled
carefully. It is easy to detect this, for the horse will show a
certain tension in his back and move with short, nappy steps.
Such horses are best lunged or led about before being mounted,
until all tension has disappeared; above all, such horses should
be saddled very carefully and the girth tightened only gradually.
It is well to loosen the girth by one or two holes a few seconds
before mounting. If horses of this type are not handled very
carefully the habit of bucking will in time become worse.

REARING

If a horse rears, the only thing to do is to ride forward,
because a horse can only rear while at a standstill. Should a
horse rear unexpectedly the rider should get hold of the mane
or grasp him round the neck in order not to lose the seat, and
to prevent him from throwing the horse over backwards by
pulling at the reins. For safety's sake it is just as well to slip
out of the irons. As soon as the horse comes down on to
his fore feet the rider must immediately let go of neck or
mane and try to ride forward with determination. It would
be the gravest mistake to hang on to the neck too long, losing
thereby the seat and all influence on the horse. Once the
horse rests on his four legs again, it is best to get his head and
neck as high up as possible, because he cannot rear if his neck
is raised. The same thing should be done if the rider anticipates
an attempt to rear, which, however, will seldom be the case.
By lowering the hands and by pressing downwards at the rein
one cannot prevent a horse from rearing !

The most awkward thing with a rearing horse is the toppling
over backwards if the horse loses the support on one or both

hind legs. Then the only thing to do is to jump clear of the horse, in order to avoid coming down under him. If one jumps too soon, however, it can happen that the horse for this very reason will fall on top of the rider, who will not have got far enough away.

RUNNING AWAY

A horse is said to 'run away' if he tears along without the rider being able to pull him up. The reason will often be that the rider has, for some reason, started to pull at the reins: in a tug-of-war the horse is always the stronger party. A horse can

very well run away with his head high up in the air and his neck bent upwards. When a rider feels that he has lost control, it is, of course, quite wrong to try and stop him by half-halts, parades or slight pulls at the reins. There is only one thing to be done: look straight ahead over the horse's ears in order to find the 'wide open spaces' towards which he can be steered, and then turn him, first on a large and then on gradually smaller circles, until he can finally be brought to a standstill in the centre. The turning must be done with the inner rein alone, and it is surprising that a runaway horse can be turned so much more easily than is generally assumed. It is very rarely that a horse will run away, with blood-shot eyes, having 'gone mad'.

PRESSING AGAINST THE WALL

Fig. 28. PRESSING AGAINST THE WALL

If a horse tries to press against a wall or tree he will always 'flex' towards the object and prop himself against it with his inner legs. (See Fig. 28.) In this case the rider must proceed exactly in the same manner as with a shying horse, that is he must bend or flex him in the opposite direction. But, whereas in the case of the shying horse, the head must be turned *away from* the object, in this case it must be turned towards it. Thus the rider makes it impossible for the horse to prop the 'inner' legs against it and can then easily drive the horse forward and away with his inner leg. Here again, the decisive thing is the flexing or bending.

STICKY HORSES

We say that a horse is 'sticky' if he tries by every means in his power to remain on the spot, with other horses, near the stable, or near a door. He may rear or buck or try to behave as if he would press the rider against some object. These attempts must be met with in the ways which have been described under their respective headings. The most important thing, however, is by all means to make the horse go forward.

If sticking to other horses or pressing towards the stable occurs after the rider has been in the saddle for some time, it can be taken as an unmistakable proof that the horse has not been properly at the aids. Such disobedience should be a serious warning to the rider to occupy himself more thoroughly with this *sine qua non* of the art of riding !

III

THE LESSONS

EXERCISES FOR LOOSENING UP

A HORSE can, of course, be mounted and ridden as soon as he comes out of the stable, but the highest concentration or complete collection cannot be asked of him immediately. Like any other living creature, the horse needs a little preparation, which we call 'loosening' or 'limbering'. According to the animal's temper and conformation this loosening up occupies a shorter or longer period. There are horses which can almost do without it, and there are others which need as much as ten minutes. A good light trot (posting) is indicated as a satisfactory means of limbering up. As soon as the horse can be put to the aids by neat and correct half-halts, the exercise has answered its purpose.

'COLLECTING' EXERCISES

These exercises comprise all those lessons which tend to further the action of the hind quarters and make them participate in an increased degree in carrying of the load by being placed more towards the centre of gravity. Half-halts and halts are examples. The decisive point in these lessons, if they are to fulfil their purpose, is that they must be carried out with sufficient action of back and legs.

THE AIDS TO 'WALK ON', 'TROT ON', AND THE 'PARADES'[1]

These aids, which are intimately connected with each other,

[1] 'Parade' is the school rider's term for 'Halt', and nothing to do with the 'parade of a regiment'. THE TRANSLATOR.

should never be discussed separately. They consist of simultaneous:

  bracing of the back,
  equal pressure of both legs
  giving—passive resistance—or taking up of the reins.

The action of the reins is therefore the regulating factor.
The aids to move on are, so to speak, in the same relation to
the aids for the 'halt' as the aids for turning left to the aids for
turning right.

Walking on, trotting on, and halting should be executed
dead straight ahead. Equal action of both legs and both reins
is, therefore, essential. If one leg or one rein acts differently
from the other a certain one-sidedness results, and, consequently, a deviation from the straight direction. On the other
hand, increased pressure of one or other rein or leg may be
necessary, in the case of innate one-sidedness in the horse,
in order to prevent deviation from the forward direction.
The rider must, therefore, always be very particular about
walking on, trotting on, or halting absolutely straight ahead.

Walking on and trotting on are taught to the rider in the
first few lessons. But whereas in those first lessons he requires
a whip or has to make use of his voice in order to make his
horse move forward, he will soon feel that if he has learnt how
to 'influence with his back' it needs very little leg pressure
and emphasis. At a later stage the trotting on from the halt is
a particularly instructive lesson because it develops the understanding of a very important axiom, i.e. that a horse must
never be taken by surprise with the aids, but that all aids must
be applied with gradually increasing emphasis. If the aids
are too crude the horse will probably canter on instead of
trotting on.

The 'halt' is more difficult to learn than walking on or
trotting on. The horse, driven forward by the rider's back
and legs, finds a resistance in the passive reins, even if they do

not pull backward; the horse is being pushed forward, but the bit does not give. The horse pulls himself up towards the front and puts more weight on his hind quarters; he will soon become lower at the rear and higher in front, the stride becoming shorter, but the action, at the same time, higher.

The difficulty for the young rider consists in the fact that during his first few lessons he was actually taught to do the wrong thing, namely: to halt his horse by pulling at the reins, because he did not then know the influence of back and loins. He would not have been able to stop his horse had he been asked to execute a correct 'parade' by back and legs. Once the rider has got into the habit of executing the 'halt' by pulling at the reins, it is, of course, very difficult for him to get rid of it. At first he will fail to see why he should make the parades or halts in any other way. It does indeed sound paradoxical to stop a forward movement by a forward driving force. To avoid doing this, however—and a rider should always bear this well in mind—is to act against the prime axiom of the art of riding: to appeal to the *whole* horse, not only to his mouth. With good-natured old horses it is certainly possible to use the reins alone; with young or lively horses, or with any horse if perfect control is desired, it would never lead anywhere, because the horse is always stronger than the man. The animal only gets into the habit of throwing his head about and leaning heavily on the bit, and he will always stop on the forehand by digging his front legs into the ground, thus rapidly wearing out his joints; in certain circumstances he may even try to bolt.

It is therefore imperative for the young rider to learn as early as possible the correct execution of the 'halt' by bracing the back and influencing with the legs. For this reason also he should be taught in the first few lessons not to let his horse step backward after a 'halt'. All horses like to do this, especially if the parade has been effected by a strong pull at the reins or if the rider, after having brought the horse to a standstill, stretches his legs away, satisfied with his marvellous feat.

There are 'full-parades' or 'halts', and 'half-parades' or 'half-halts'. The full-parade serves to bring the horse to a standstill, regardless of the gait, whereas half-parades effect only a shortening of the stride of the particular gait or a change to the walk. A half-parade can also be executed by the before-mentioned influences *within* the particular gait, without slowing down the pace, but increasing the collection with a resulting higher action. If a half-parade does not go through the whole horse, i.e. if the horse does not answer to it or not to the required degree, it must be repeated. A full-parade, like-wise, will seldom result right away in a perfect standstill and must be repeated as often as necessary until it finally leads to success. As the emphasis with which a full or half-parade is executed must correspond to the sensibility of the horse, there can hardly be a difference as regards the execution of the half-parade and that of the full-parade.

It is obvious that the emphasis with which a full-parade must be given in order to come to a halt out of a strong trot, must be greater—or, rather, *more frequent*—than the pressure for a half-parade leading from a middle trot to a collected trot. On the other hand, the pressure for the half-parade, when changing from the extended trot to the walk, must be stronger, *or more frequent,* than that for a full-parade from the walk to the standstill.

Half-parades should, therefore, always be given before asking something new of the horse, i.e. before changing the direction or the pace or gait. A half-parade is the 'attention !' for the horse, and all these half-parades are executed in the same way: by driving the horse from rear to front into the passively resisting hand. The more frequently a horse is given the half-parade the more attentive will he be and the better will the rider have him under control. These frequent half-halts will gradually lead to a stage where their execution

will become more and
more subtle, until
finally the rider will
have but to *think* of
the half-parade, there-
by automatically
bracing his loins, for
the horse to become
immediately attentive.

The young rider
must not think that it
is possible to arrive
at such control of his
own body, and his
horse's, by just a few
casual exercises ! The
task is like a game of
patience, and must be
continued for days,
weeks, months and
even years until per-
fection is reached.
The neater, finer and
more subtle a half-
halt is executed the
more complete will be
the harmony between
man and mount and
the more perfectly
will the full-parades
'go through'. At the

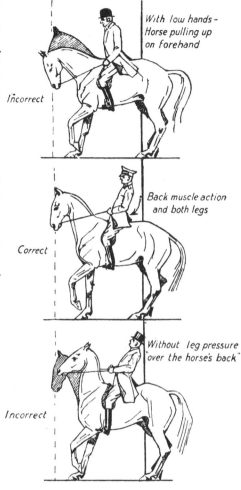

Incorrect — With low hands -
Horse pulling up
on forehand

Correct — Back muscle action
and both legs

Incorrect — Without leg pressure
"over the horse's back"

Fig. 29. THE HALT

Compare Plate 4 and Fig. 7, page 21

same time the seat of the rider will itself gradually improve;
he will follow more and more closely the movements of his
horse, and his aids will be given with more subtle feel, until
finally they are imperceptible to the onlooker.

WALK AND TROT

The walk and the trot are gaits with regular foot-fall. Their explanation during the ordinary course of instruction is usually sufficient, but it must be emphasized here that every rider should at all times be conscious of the fact that he must never ride 'just at a walk' or 'just at a trot' but always:

At the walk:

(1) the long, extended walk with loose reins or
(2) the collected walk with reins taut, the horse walking in a lively manner but without haste.

At the trot:

(1) the ordinary trot, or
(2) the collected trot, or
(3) the medium trot, or
(4) the extended trot.

The more often the rider changes the pace the better, and the more often will he remember that he must maintain a definite pace and not relapse into some undefined jog which the horse offers to go. If the horse gradually slows down, it is always the rider's fault. He has obviously fallen asleep.

The rider has an opportunity of showing his purpose and energy by always *riding forward*. He must always dictate the pace by urging the horse on. It is often said of a rider that he does not ride with sufficient energy, by which most people mean that he gives too much with his hands. The reproach is only justified if the rider has forgotten at the same time to urge his horse on. Be his hands ever so soft and subtle—if he drives the horse sufficiently forward—and rather few of all riders do—then his riding is not without energy. Energy lies in the 'forward' and not in the 'backward'.

RIDING 'IN POSITION RIGHT OR LEFT'

A horse is said to be in straight position if his spinal column from the poll to the tail forms a straight line. If it is bent to one side or the other, one says that the horse is in 'position left' or 'position right'. In 'position left', the centre of the circle of which the crescent formed by the spinal column is an arc, is on the left, and in 'position right' this centre is on the right. The side to which the imaginary centre lies is called the 'inner side',[1] regardless of whether this side is towards the inside of the riding school or not. The 'inner side' of the horse can therefore be on the near side if we ride on the 'left hand'; but it will be on the off side (towards the wall) if we ride on the left hand in 'position right'.

The lateral flexion which should go throughout the whole length of the horse begins at the poll and continues all through neck and back. The maximum of such flexion is reached when the horse can adapt itself in the volte to a circle of six feet diameter.

A horse can also be flexed or positioned unharmoniously so that the flexion does not form a regular arch from the neck to the tail.

Equal, harmonious lateral flexion can only be obtained if the horse has first of all been properly put to the aids.

In general, people fuss much too much about 'flexing' and 'riding in position'. After all, the purpose of riding is, as a rule, to *go forward*, to get ahead; hence, more importance should be attached to riding straight forward.

The young rider should be taught very particularly to ride 'straight on' and forward and to develop his feel for whether his horse is really going perfectly straight and in a straight-forward position.

In turns and at the canter the horse cannot be quite straight; consequently, it is necessary for the rider to occupy himself

[1] See explanation in Translator's footnote, p. 19.

sooner or later with 'riding in position'. (See also Plate 3 and sketch, p. 41.)

The lesson for flexing, or 'positioning', a horse in the correct way is a comparatively complicated one, because the rider must influence simultaneously with back, weight, both legs and both reins, and he must act differently towards the right from towards the left. He must think of his pelvic bones and his loins, his knees and his heels; he must properly displace his weight, and he must not collapse in the hips. It will, therefore, be some time before the young rider can flex or 'position' his horse correctly. He must first learn and try out the perfect co-operation of all his influences by turns on the spot (pivots on the haunches and on the fore legs). Although he may have understood theoretically the points which matter, endless patience and practice will be needed to acquire the feel for these various influences.

The rider's inner leg forms the fulcrum or pivot. Although it remains passive, acting, as it were, only as a gentle restrainer, it must not be stretched away from the horse's side; without this inner leg it is impossible to bend or flex the horse, all the other influences only causing him to side-step.

First Phase:

The horse is pulled up with a half-parade.

Second Phase:

Flexing begins around the rider's inner leg.
The centre of gravity is shifted towards the inside (of the circle).
Inner hip and inner pelvic bone are pressed forward.
Inner heel and inner knee are lowered.
The outer leg presses or pushes the hind quarters towards the inside.
The inner rein is gently taken up.
The outer rein gives a little. A horse which has been

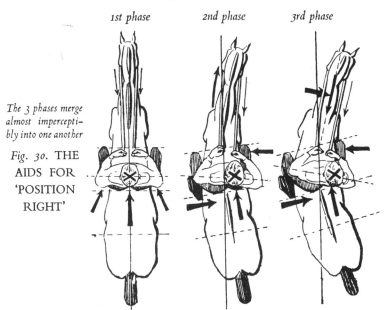

1st phase   2nd phase   3rd phase

The 3 phases merge almost imperceptibly into one another

Fig. 30. THE AIDS FOR 'POSITION RIGHT'

properly put to the aids, will now try to lengthen his neck to keep contact with the rider's hand. This going forward or giving of the outer rein comes quite automatically by the rider's shoulders turning a little towards the inside, without, however, imparting this turn to the hips. The outer rein can also give a little by slightly turning the fist so that the little finger moves a trifle towards the horse's mouth.

Third Phase:

As soon as a little flexion is obtained the outer rein is likewise gently taken up again. It will now—the horse's neck being already bent—act in the direction of the chord of the arc, thus increasing the flexion. To shift the outer hand across the withers would be utterly wrong. The rider's back, weight and both legs, as well as the inner rein, continue their influences as before.

The most important influence is the displacement of the weight. (A cyclist makes a turn more by shifting his weight towards the inside than by actually steering with the handle-bars.) Without it the whole movement would not be har-monious, because the rider must always endeavour to keep his centre of gravity in co-ordination with that of the horse. If we want the horse to flex along its whole length we must make him bring his centre of gravity towards the inside, and if the horse is thus bending around the inner leg the rider must necessarily sit accordingly, i.e. his inner pelvic bone and hip must be pushed forward, his inner leg in contact with the horse, close behind the girth, and his outer leg a little further back, about a hand to the rear of the girth.

It is difficult to say whether, with the rein influences, the giving of the outer rein or the pulling up of the inner, are of greater importance in Phase (2). It depends largely on the degree of the horse's training and sensitiveness. In no case will the rider be able to obtain proper flexion by merely taking up the inner rein. Sooner or later every horse will revolt against such unilateral influence. With young and high-spirited horses the giving of the outer hand is certainly more important than the taking up of the inner.

In Phase (3) as soon as a certain flexion towards the inside is obtained, both reins are taken up, the outer one a little more than the inner one. Whilst the inner rein should act softly, just sufficiently to maintain contact, the outer rein should increase the flexion and fortify the 'position'. Wrong flexion or resistance in the neck or any kind of bad habit during the flexing are mostly brought about by too much use of the inner rein rather than by too much use of the outer one. If the horse tries to throw his head about or disobeys the aids, or presses towards the inside of the school, he must be driven forward and properly put to the aids again. For the rider to examine and criticize himself during the 'riding in position' is more difficult than it is in most other lessons. Even if mirrors are fixed in the riding school many riders will make mistakes by exaggerating the seat or by collapsing at the hips. A rider has no chance of testing his feel for proper flexion until he can make practical use of such flexions on circles, turns, voltes, serpentines, at the canter, and in turns on the spot, mainly in the pivot on the haunches. It is often recommended, wrongly, that the outer shoulder should be drawn back a little when riding in position. The point of this is that many people are so stiff that if they move their outer shoulder backward they move also their outer hip at the same time. The outer hip, however, should not be moved backward, but the *inner hip should be pushed forward*—not the same thing at all ! Apart from that, anybody can move hips and shoulders independently, and on horseback should be so supple and relaxed that he actually does so. If a rider is stiff, his stiffness should not be increased by such ill-conceived advice. The outer shoulder must not be taken back, but thrust a trifle forward. The rider will then have the horse's neck straight in front of him, at right angles to his own shoulders.

'Counter position' is the expression for that position of the horse which is opposed to the hand on which the horse is being ridden, i.e. 'position left' if riding 'on the right hand', and vice versa. A 'counter lesson' is an exercise in 'counter position'. Riding in counter position as well as all counter lessons are particularly valuable because they are contrary to the horse's habits. The rider is forced to apply all the various aids with the utmost correctness and precision. He must thoroughly concentrate upon the emphasis of the various influences, for the horse will not assist him in executing these lessons, by anticipating them at the first indications of the aids by sheer force of habit.

TURNS ON THE SPOT

Pivoting on the spot is indispensable as a preparation for riding 'in position', on the circle, in the volte and for cantering on. The influences required for these later exercises can only be learned at the standstill, as they are different for the right hand side and for the left and because the young rider is preoccupied with keeping his balance when the horse is moving. In pivoting on the spot he can concentrate on the manner in which he should apply the aids and on the emphasis to be given to them. Also, he can readily find out if and how the horse reacts. These pivoting exercises should, therefore, be taken up during intervals in the very first lessons. There will, later on, be little or no difficulties in flexing a horse into the correct position, once the feel for these unilateral influences has been acquired.

For the pivots to be executed correctly it is imperative that they be carried out step by step. The rider must make a pause after each step in order to examine whether that step was correct or not.

This procedure and nothing but this procedure will develop his feel. This procedure and nothing but this procedure will make it clear to him whether his influences have had the desired effect, whether they have been given with the necessary emphasis and whether they were co-ordinated or not. If the young rider thinks that there is nothing to it and that in pivoting he can at once execute several consecutive steps he will miss a splendid opportunity of acquiring 'feel' and will never be able to execute perfectly correct turns in motion.

In general, the pivot on the haunches is considered rather difficult. Consequently it is dreaded and the necessary practice is seldom devoted to it. Most people begin much too late to execute it. But if the rider cannot make perfect pivots on the haunches towards both sides, it can be taken for granted that he can neither ride a correct volte, nor put his horse in a correct position for cantering on.

THE PIVOT ON THE SHOULDERS

In pivoting on the shoulders, the horse must turn round one fore foot, in the about-turn right round the right, and in the about-turn left round the left foot. During the pivot the horse must be adequately flexed, e.g. in turning about right in 'position right' (see Fig. 31, I), and in 'counter position' (see Fig. 31, II). For the training of the horse, the pivots on the shoulders are considered to be of little value because they more or less liberate the haunches, bringing the horse more on to the forehand. But they are valuable as a test for the horse's leg-obedience and to educate him to it.

For the young rider, again, the pivot on the shoulders is an indispensable means to the development of his feel and as a preparation for the pivot on the haunches. It is not necessary that the horse be always turned about completely and it is very instructive if, after two or three steps, he is brought back into the original position. Each pivot on the shoulders begins with a half-halt in order to secure the horse's attention and for the rider to readjust his seat. The horse should then be flexed towards the inside of the circle on which the pivot is to be carried out. At first this will present difficulties, for it is just these very pivots which are to teach the young rider the feel for the way he can bend or flex his horse. The rider then presses with his inner leg directly or close behind the girth, causing the hind legs to make one step sideways. The outer leg, having contact with the horse's body about a hand behind the girth, restrains, or, as it were, catches this side movement and limits it. The horse must stand perfectly still after each step, being firmly held between both the rider's legs!

The rider must not attempt the next step unless he is satisfied that the execution of this last was perfectly correct and that his influences were exercised in complete co-ordination and with the necessary emphasis.

In the *pivot on the shoulders with opposite or counter flexion* (II) the horse is flexed to the side to which the hind legs are made to step. The side-stepping of the hind legs is now effected by the rider's outer leg which should be

approximately a hand behind the girth. Each step must
now be caught by the inner leg.

Many riders act unconsciously with their hands. This can
easily be spotted because the horse tries to creep backwards,
shakes his head or contracts other bad habits. Under no
circumstances must the horse step forward or backward; if
he tries to step forward he must be checked and if he tries to
crawl back he must be pressed forward with back and both
legs so that he remains perfectly quiet on the spot.

For the rider the instructive part of the pivot on the shoulder
is that he not only effects side-stepping with one leg, but
exercises *unequal* influences with both legs. The side movement which is caused by the one leg must be limited by the
other. And just as he can catch or limit this side movement,
he can also prevent it by counter pressure. It is by this play
of the forces and influences that his feel is developed.

At the same time, it is an excellent means of improving the
position of the legs. The pivot on the shoulder cannot be
executed correctly unless the legs have sound, close contact
with the horse. A rider who has never felt the effect of leg
pressure and who does not go to the trouble of testing it
frequently can hardly have the correct feel for the position of
his legs. If, on the other hand, the feel has by frequent practice been refined to such a degree that the rider not only feels
that a step has been carried out, but that he *anticipated* it—felt
that the horse was just about to do it—then he has the means
to test his own leg position. The refinement of this feel
enables him to tell whether his legs are in the right position or
not, and he will not need anybody to confirm it. This is part
of the importance which the pivot on the shoulders has for
the education of the rider.

THE PIVOT ON THE HAUNCHES

In the pivot on the haunches, the horse should turn round
the inner hind leg. This pivot is always executed in the

corresponding flexion (about-turn right in 'position right' and about-turn left in 'position left'). For the training of the horse, the pivot on the haunches is valuable as a preparation for passing corners in the school, for the volte, for collection and for all side movements. For the rider it is indispensable in developing his feel and the co-ordination of unilateral influences. The first three steps of this pivot are easier to execute

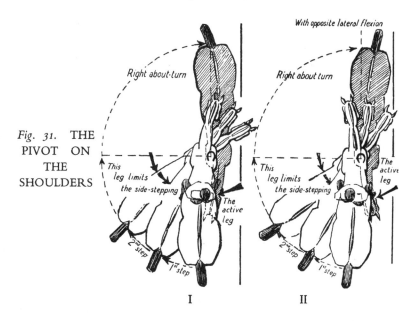

Fig. 31. THE PIVOT ON THE SHOULDERS

than the following ones. The reason is that during the first three steps the horse can, without difficulty, let the inner hind leg stand as it is; but when he has turned as much as about one-third of the whole pivot he wants to straighten out his hind foot, which has assumed a somewhat awkward twist, and he will try either to step to the side or forward or backward. Consequently the rider will probably execute the first three steps much more easily, and it is well to let him practise at first only one, two or three steps. Each time the horse is brought back into the original position step by step, by pivoting in the other direction.

After the word of command for the 'pivot on the haunches' the rider must be given ample time for its preparation. Although the preparation was perhaps not so important in the pivot on the shoulders, because it did not really matter to which side the horse was flexed, for the pivot on the haunches it is most important.

This preparation begins with a half-halt perfectly straight

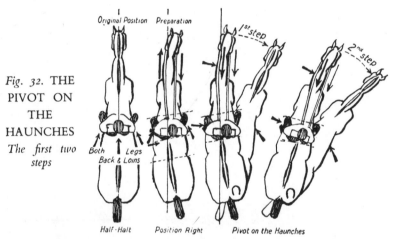

Fig. 32. THE PIVOT ON THE HAUNCHES
The first two steps

ahead (Phase 1). The horse is then flexed (Phase 2). When beginning the pivot proper, the rider must sit with his weight well towards the inside and with the inner pelvic bone pushed forward, the inner leg at the girth, the outer approximately a hand behind it. By increased pressure the outer rein and the outer leg cause the horse to step sideways.

The inner rein is in soft contact and is only concerned with maintaining flexion.

The inner leg limits the side movement, i.e. it prevents the horse from doing more than one step at a time.

The horse should stand still after each step, firmly enclosed between the rider's legs. The rider must not proceed with the next step until he is satisfied that the execution of the previous

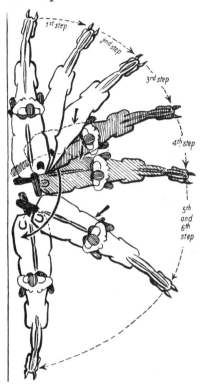

step was correct and that all influences have been exercised in full harmony and with the necessary emphasis. If the horse steps forward or crawls back (which, by the way, is the worse of the two!) or if he pokes his head out or otherwise shows that he 'doesn't like it' it is pretty certain that the rider has disturbed him by some incorrect influence. It is wrong to believe that stretching the legs away or giving him the reins would quieten him. The only thing to do is to put him properly to the aids with back muscles and both legs, and not execute the next step before he has come to a perfect standstill!

If during the pivot the horse crawls back it may

Fig. 33. THE PIVOT ON THE HAUNCHES

Positions of critical phases are shaded

become necessary for the rider to interrupt this lesson and to move on. The rider must have acquired the definite feel that *going forward* is, in this as in all other circumstances, the decisive factor !

As soon as the rider can proficiently turn the horse three steps and back again, it is time to let him execute the further steps. The outer leg must in the following steps exert more

9

pressure than in the preceding steps, because after the third or fourth step, the horse will try to side-step towards the outside. The inner leg must, of course, allow the horse gradually to turn his haunches as indicated by the long arrow in the figure on p. 129.

But even now the inner leg must continue to catch each single step and must limit it; the horse should, therefore, not turn slowly and gradually after the third or fourth step, but a short, yet definite interval should follow each single step.

Do not think that the horse can be 'pulled round' by the inner or leading rein!

After completion of the pivot the horse is again put straight on the track. Under no circumstances must he be allowed to crawl backwards.

The development of the pivot on the haunches from the walk is most instructive. If the rider is not yet proficient in putting his horse to the aids while at a standstill, he can develop the first step of the pivot from the walk, while simultaneously coming to the halt, making good use thereby of the forward movement of the horse. He must, however, master the unilateral influences to a certain extent and the halt must really be effected by back muscles and leg action.

The rider has not completely mastered the pivot on the haunches until he is in a position to execute it at any given spot in the riding school, that is, also in the centre of the school without the help of the track or the wall. If he can do it then he has acquired sufficient feel to enable him to execute turns in motion, to flex his horse and to canter on correctly. As long as he does not fully master the pivot on the haunches his feel is certainly not developed to such an extent that he can do correct turns in motion.

TO 'CANTER ON'

We distinguish between 'cantering on the right' (or leading on the off fore) and 'cantering on the left' (or leading on the near fore). In the canter to the right, the horse is flexed right and his right hand pair of legs are in advance; in the canter left the horse is flexed to the left and the left legs advance. The foot-fall is, of course, entirely different from that of the walk or the trot.

Mostly, the young rider is allowed to do a little cantering in the very first lessons in order to increase his pleasure in riding and add to his enthusiasm. Turning the corners at the canter will also give him a certain feel for balance. In the first lessons, little importance is attached to the correctness of the canter. School horses will mostly canter on at the instructor's voice. But to sit well at the canter and to follow this movement can only be learned with the correct 'cantering on.' The same was the case with the trot, for there, too, the pupil learned to follow the movement and go with the horse only when he had been taught to walk on or trot on by means of correct back-muscle action.

In order to canter on it is not only necessary to make a half-halt, thus attracting the animal's attention, but to be flexed left or right, according to which side we decide to canter. Before cantering on there must be no doubt whatever in the rider's mind as to which is to be the leading leg, and the aids must be given accordingly.

The aid for cantering on does not begin from the normal or straight seat but from the seat which the rider must assume if he wishes to flex his horse either towards the left or towards the right. Consequently, the inner hip is pushed forward, the inner leg has close contact at the girth, the outer one being approximately a hand behind the girth. If the rider now quietly urges his horse forward with his back and both legs, at the same time giving with the reins, the horse will trot on in 'position left' or 'position right'.

In order to put the horse into a canter and not into a trot, the cadence of the foot-fall must be altered. This is mainly effected by a very energetic forward push of the inner pelvic bone and by the unilateral bracing of the back muscles. In this connexion both legs press the horse forward (the inner at the girth, the outer one half a hand behind the girth). Both reins must give equally in order to let the movement come out forward. The pressure on the inner side can be a little increased by a slight restraint of the outer reins.

The decisive factor is the unilateral back-muscle action. At a very highly developed stage (Haute École), this back-muscle action alone will be sufficient not only to make a horse canter on but also to change the lead during the canter. Since back-muscle aids are inconceivable without the supporting or restraining influences of the legs, the gradual change from coarser to refined aids will hardly be perceptible.

Cantering on is taught in different ways. One can make a horse canter on either by the whip or by the voice or even by a click of the tongue. It is often said that the horse should be flexed towards the outside so as to give him more freedom in the shoulders (in which case the flexion would be something like an 'S'). Again, riders are often recommended to canter on only by means of the outer leg. All such advice is misleading.

A rider canters on correctly if he sits in complete harmony, i.e. as the horse's movements require. All doubts can be removed by testing oneself. If you cannot feel whether your horse canters on on the wrong leg, then you may rest assured that your seat is wrong. This requires a little explanation.

The horse quite naturally bends a little towards the right when leading on the off fore and to the left when leading on the near fore, and not only is the inner pair of legs in advance and groping forward, but the whole of his muscles, including those of the inward bent back, work in accordance with this flexion. If the rider now endeavours to follow this movement, and stick to the saddle as he has learned to do at the trot (see p. 12), he must push his inner pelvic bone and his hips forward by a unilateral bracing of the back. If he has properly learned to do that he can stick to the saddle at the canter with the same ease as at the trot.

If the rider pushes the inner side forward and the horse tries to canter on, leading on the opposite leg, the rider would no more be sitting in harmony, and could not therefore remain glued to the saddle. The rider must feel with his buttocks whether the horse is leading on the wrong leg, for the horse will try to seat him differently from the way he wishes to sit. Whereas he wants to push his right hip and right pelvic bone forward, the horse pushes his left hip and left pelvic bone forward. Obviously a kind of 'rotating' movement results, and this he *must* feel under his buttocks, because it prevents him from remaining glued to the saddle. When the rider has been taught to pay attention to this the feel for it will soon develop.

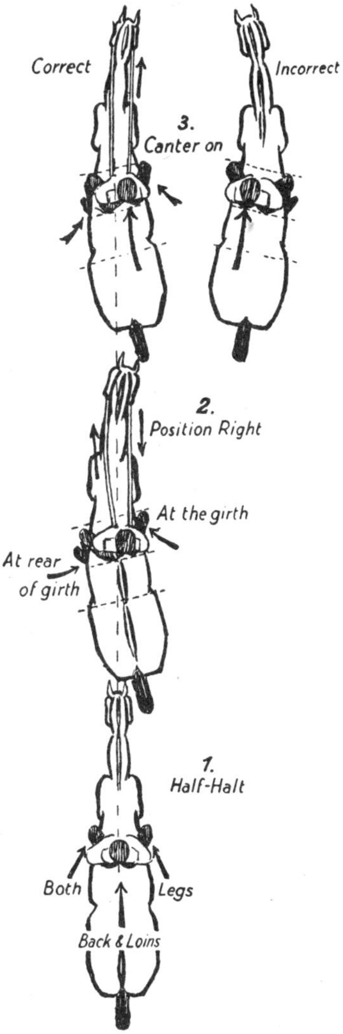

Once the rider, for himself, has learned to canter on properly, he can alternatively canter on on the right or the left

Fig. 34. 'CANTER-ON' ON THE RIGHT

leg, and can also teach his horse the proper way to canter on.

Cantering on is best done from the walk, either from a volte or from a corner of the riding school, until the rider has arrived at some proficiency in this exercise. It is easier for him to assume the correct seat at the walk and all horses canter on more easily in a turn (corner or volte).

With advanced education, proper care should be taken that the horse's hind quarters are not brought too much to the inside and that the horse canters on perfectly straight, on a single track.

THE CANTER[1]

One should never ride 'just a canter', but either a quiet working canter, a collected canter, a medium canter, or an extended canter or gallop. The differences between these paces should be strictly observed, and the rider should remind himself, by frequent changes of pace, not to relapse into some undefinable sort of a cantering jog.

The feel at the canter is entirely different from that at the trot. The canter is a sort of soft, swinging movement caused by a different cadence of the foot-fall. Riders who can well go with and into the movement of the horse at the trot have still to learn to follow the movement at the canter. There are riders who can do the one well, but not the other. 'Sticking' or 'being glued' to the saddle depends on the manner of cantering on and can only be done by learning the correct manner of cantering on. Altogether it is very important for the rider to acquire the true feel for the movement of the horse at the canter (see sketches, p. 135).

At the canter the rider involuntarily partakes of the up and down movement of the horse's shoulders and hind quarters. As the horse is in the first phase high in front, most riders lean a little forward and invariably lift their buttocks out of the saddle. That, of course, is wrong. And when in the third

[1] The German language has only one expression for this gait: 'The Gallop'. 'Gallop' in German includes, therefore, everything from a slow school canter to the actual racing gallop. THE TRANSLATOR.

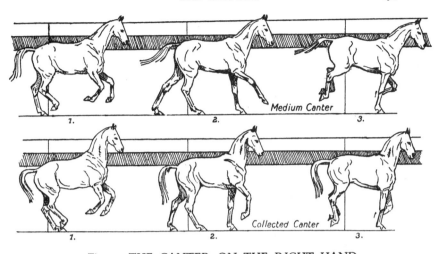

Fig. 35. THE CANTER ON THE RIGHT HAND

After the 3rd phase there follows a phase of complete suspension.   The border in both drawing is at the same height from the track

phase, the horse is lower in front, the rider tends to lean a little backward.[1]

The faster the canter, the faster the movement and the longer the stride.   The shorter the turns we wish to ride at the canter, and the more we desire to have the horse in hand, the more reliable must be the putting to the aids, the more collected must be the canter and the more must the weight be transferred to the haunches.   In the collected canter the hind quarters are lowered and the shoulders are relatively high.

The expression 'shortened canter', which was formerly quite ·common, led to the erroneous belief that the criterion of this gait lay in the shortness of the stride.   For this reason we say to-day 'collected canter'.   At the same time, we still speak of a 'shortened gallop' or 'shortened canter' when we mean that

[1] A photograph should be taken during the 2nd phase, i.e. when three legs are on the ground. At this instance the rider usually sits best, neither leaning forward, nor backward.

the natural, free strides have been wrongly shortened by pulling at the reins.

At the canter the horse is collected by half-halts, just as he is at the trot. But most riders relapse into the mistake of pulling at the reins even more at the canter than at the trot. The young rider can avoid this mistake only by endeavouring to obtain collection at the canter by frequently cantering on.

When cantering on from the walk, the action of the first stride will mostly be a pretty high one; but this collection is invariably lost after the second or third stride. The reason is that although the rider has applied the correct aids at the beginning, he has entirely forgotten to renew them with each subsequent stride. As at the trot, where by his back-muscle action the rider sticks to the saddle, urges the horse forward and collects him, so at the canter he must collect the horse and drive him forward by continuously renewing all his aids at each and every stride. With advanced training these aids will gradually become more and more refined until finally a unilateral bracing of the back will be sufficient.

Many riders understand how to stick to the saddle at the trot and how to put their horse to the aids, but few have ever learned that unilateral back influence is just as important at the canter as equal or bilateral back action is at the trot.

TURNS IN MOTION

By 'turns' we mean any kind of change of direction: turning left or right, half-left or half-right, passing corners, riding on a circle, voltes and serpentines. Correct turns can only be executed if the rider has acquired a good feel for co-ordination and adequate emphasis of unilateral influences by turning at the halt.

At the beginning, the docile and placid horse on which the rider is taught to balance will probably do all the turns by himself, i.e. without any special aids. The experience of the first few lessons teach the rider that when turning a corner he is more or less forced to displace his weight towards the inside in order to avoid sliding off on the outside. In riding a horse, just as in riding a bicycle, a turn is executed mainly by shifting the weight towards the inside of the turn.

Each turn should be prepared for and initiated by a half-halt. It secures attention of the horse and, at the same time, corrects the rider's seat. The horse is then flexed towards the side to which the turn is to be made; the rider shifts his centre of gravity towards the inside of the circle or arc of a circle, his inner leg at the girth and the outer behind it.

The aid for turning must only begin when the horse has assumed the proper lateral flexion. The inner or leading rein 'leads into' the turn and is merely concerned with softly maintaining this flexion. The outer rein and the outer leg effect, as in the pivot on the haunches, the deviation from the straight line and determine the bend of the turn.

The inner leg, again, just as in the pivot on the haunches, is the restraining one, limiting the turn and at the same time driving forward.

Both legs and both reins are active, but with varied pressure and emphasis, according to the sensitiveness of the horse. In a correctly executed turn the hoof-prints of the hind legs must follow the hoof-prints of the front legs precisely as shown in the figure on p. 138. In a freshly raked school the rider can easily see if he has made a turn correctly.

Various circumstances, however, can cause the horse either to press towards the inside or towards the outside, perhaps with the hind quarters only, and this need not necessarily be the fault of the rider.

In a covered riding school all horses have a tendency to round off the corners; consequently, the rider must be more active with his inner leg in order to press the horse more into the corner. It would, in this case, be the smaller mistake if the hind legs moved on a larger circle than the fore legs, the

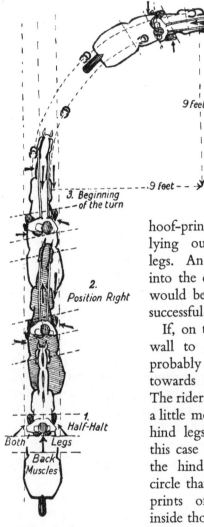

Fig. 36. THE
TURN IN
MOTION

*The 'lean-to' of the
horse (owing to the cen-
trifugal force) is omitted
in the drawing so as not
to complicate it. (See
page 41)*

9 feet

.9 feet

3. Beginning
of the turn

2.
Position Right

1.
Half-Halt
Both   Legs
Back
Muscles

hoof-prints of the hind legs thus
lying outside those of the fore
legs. An attempt to press the horse
into the corner with the inner rein
would be wrong and certainly un-
successful.

If, on the other hand, there is no
wall to guide the horse, he will
probably throw his hind quarters
towards the outside of the turn.
The rider must then use his outer leg
a little more in order to prevent the
hind legs from swinging out. In
this case it is the smaller mistake if
the hind legs describe a smaller
circle than the front legs, the hoof-
prints of the hind legs falling
inside those of the front legs.

Most riders believe that they can ride turns correctly at a
much too early stage of their training ! It is very difficult to
ride an absolutely correct volte, i.e. one in which hind legs
and front legs move on one track; it requires an exceedingly

fine feel for correct emphasis and co-ordination of influences. The rider who is convinced that he has acquired the necessary amount of feel can easily test the fact by trying to ride two voltes at one and the same spot on a single track. If this test is carried out in a freshly-raked school the hoof-prints will show a most surprising re-sult !

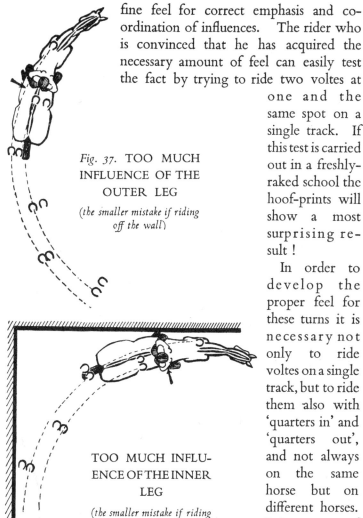

Fig. 37. TOO MUCH INFLUENCE OF THE OUTER LEG

(the smaller mistake if riding off the wall)

TOO MUCH INFLU-ENCE OF THE INNER LEG

(the smaller mistake if riding along the wall)

In order to develop the proper feel for these turns it is necessary not only to ride voltes on a single track, but to ride them also with 'quarters in' and 'quarters out', and not always on the same horse but on different horses. It is a matter of course that the horse, after each turn, be put perfectly straight again.

In the 'change of hand on two circles' the horse must be put straight shortly before reaching the centre of the school and must be flexed in the opposite direction when going on the other circle. 'Change of hand in the circle' should always be ridden in such a way that the change is made in the direction towards the closed side of the circle and not towards the open one (see Fig. 42). Shortly before reaching the centre of the circle the horse must be put straight. For an instant he remains perfectly straight and at right angles to the short wall of the school. With the next step he must be re-flexed. It is important to observe the correct shape of the S-bend, not only for reasons of pleasantness, but because unless the rider forces himself to make both arcs of the change equally big, he will not apply the correct aids for turning. He can only give the correct aids and impart his will to the horse if he is clearly conscious of what line he wants to ride.

The same rules apply to the 'serpentine'. Here too, the horse must be properly flexed and put straight again before re-flexing towards the other side. The flexion must go from the poll to the tail, right through the whole horse. This is the really important and instructive part of riding a serpentine, both for the horse and the rider.

'NARROWING THE CIRCLE' AND 'WIDENING THE CIRCLE'

The purpose of these two lessons is to make rider and horse acquainted with the influences by which a circle can either be widened or narrowed. They are carried out similarly to all other turns with 'quarters in' or 'quarters out'.

When narrowing the circle the horse is gradually led on a spiral towards the centre of the circle, the forehand, through the influence of the outer rein, being gradually led towards the centre and the hind quarters gradually brought in by the outer leg.

In widening the circle, the outer rein and the inner leg gradually lead the horse towards the outside. It would be wrong and contrary to all rules if the rider endeavoured to lead the horse towards the outside by pressing him with the inner rein across neck and withers.

Both exercises are difficult for the young rider and should not be attempted too early. The rider must already have a straight and confirmed seat and plenty of feel for the co-operation of his aids and influences. It is well if at the beginning the young rider tries, at every turn, to make his horse do three or four steps with his hind quarters to the outside or the inside. But he must not attempt to make more than four steps, otherwise it would easily involve him in a wrong seat and a certain rigidity.

THE 'REIN-BACK'

The aids to rein-back correspond to the aids for walking on, trotting on and the halt (see p. 113). Back muscles and both legs press the horse forward, but the reins act in the opposite direction and thereby cause the horse at the very moment when he is prepared to step forward, not to step forward but to step backward. Pulling at the reins without adequate leg-pressure is quite wrong. We should not pull at the mouth but get the whole of the horse to move backwards.

If the horse does not willingly rein back when these aids are applied, it means that he has not been properly put to the aids. So first of all he must be put to them and each rein-back must be preceded by a half-halt.

When making a horse step backwards we should always know precisely how many steps we want him to take—one, two, three or four. And we must not then allow him to take more steps than we intend. A rider who does not do this has not only forgotten that the rein-back must be limited by his forward driving influences, but has most probably relapsed into pulling at the reins.

If a horse is properly reined back, being neatly at the aids, he will neither throw his head about, nor raise it or lower it, or lean on the bit, or step sideways with his hind legs. If he does any one of these things the rider has reliable proof that his influences have been without feel and not in co-ordination and that his horse has not been properly at the aids.

It is particularly instructive to move on forward without coming to a standstill, immediately from the last step backwards.

The rein-back is the severest and most positive test of the co-ordination between driving and restraining influences. The young rider should therefore not attempt to execute it before being able to execute a correct, clean 'parade'.

'BENDING' AND 'FLEXING'

'Bending' and 'flexing' belong to the education of the horse. They must be mentioned, because sooner or later every rider will be faced with the question of what is meant by these expressions.

Just as any man can supple his joints and muscles by physical exercises, it is quite natural that the horse in its training should be loosened and suppled by similar exercises. Bending or flexing lessons, serve as a preparation for all side movements and the 'shoulder in' (see p. 143).

In 'bending', the horse is bent over his whole length just as when moving 'in position' (see Figs. 38 and 39), but the forehand only is off the track at the side, while the hind quarters continue *on the track,* so that the inner hind leg steps between the hoof-prints of the front legs (whereas when riding in position the outer hind leg steps between the hoof-prints of the fore legs).

In 'shoulder in' (see the above Figs.) the horse is positioned as in 'bending', but he is bent more in the ribs and his fore legs are, therefore, off the track so that the inner hind leg follows the outer fore leg.

In 'flexing', the neck and head of the horse are turned a little more than in bending.

These lessons can be done during the halt as well as in motion. The influences are the same as described for 'riding in position'. Young riders should not try these exercises but should be satisfied with 'riding in position', for the temptation merely to pull the head and neck round is too great.

Many horses have rather stiff jaws. But there are very few from which, with proper training, the required lateral flexion cannot be obtained. If this flexion is not obtainable, the reason in most cases is that much too much pulling has been done at their necks and mouths. In the stable and in feeding, one can observe that such horses usually are very well able to turn the head quite comfortably to both sides.

In most cases, however, it is much more effective to put them properly to the aids than to 'bend' or 'flex' them, especially if these exercises are not carried out very carefully (which is, unfortunately, very seldom done). It is more effective also for the simple reason that it applies, with a greater probability, to the whole of the horse. Also it eliminates the danger of the horse throwing himself on to one or other shoulder (which often happens with 'bending' or 'flexing'), thus creating a new source of stiffness, rigidity or one-sidedness.

LESSONS ON TWO TRACKS

In the lessons on a single track the hind legs follow the hoof-prints of the fore legs. If the horse is put aslant to the direction of motion he goes on two tracks. The tracks, however, must not be so far apart from each other that the regular cadence of the steps is thereby impaired, or injuries to legs and tendons may easily result.

All lessons on two tracks require a very firm seat and a lot of feel. To the beginner they can do more harm than good. The lessons on two tracks comprise all side movements and 'leg yielding'.

In 'leg yielding', the horse's head is turned towards the side

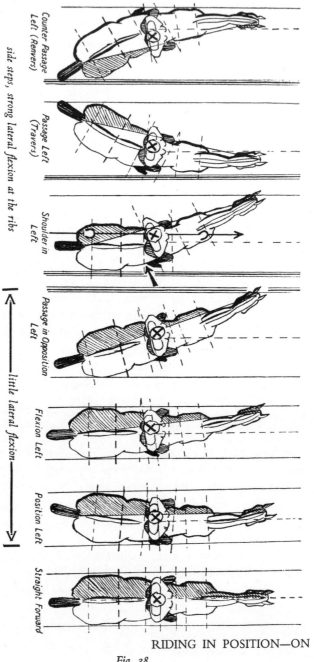

Counter Passage Left (Renvers)

Passage Left (Travers)

Shoulder in Left

Passage in Opposition Left

Flexion Left

Position Left

Straight Forward

side steps, strong lateral flexion at the ribs

|← little lateral flexion →|

In the 'shoulder in' the horse cannot be flexed off the wall more than shown in this drawing, because more flexion in the ribs is impossible. The outer leg must act with emphasis or else the hind quarters would swing sideways and the hind feet would side step as in 'leg-yielding'

RIDING IN POSITION—ON

Fig. 38.

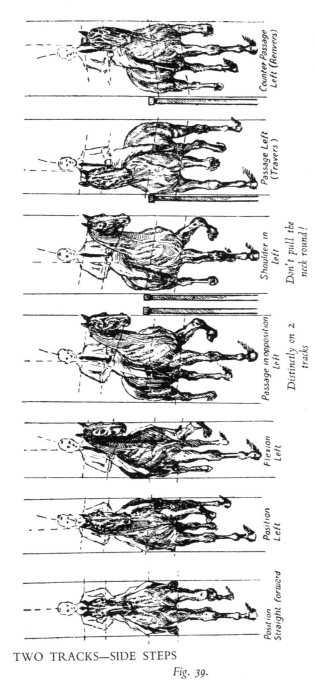

Position
Straight forward

Position
Left

Flexion
Left

Passage in opposition
Left

Distinctly on 2
tracks

Shoulder in
Left

Don't pull the
neck round!

Passage Left
(Travers)

Counter Passage
Left (Renvers)

Each rider comes straight on toward the onlooker! If the thin lines are eliminated all riders seem to sit perfectly straight—no collapsed hips. Although flexed, the horses, above all, go forward, not sideways. Swing and action are to be maintained; if they are lost the whole work is useless

TWO TRACKS—SIDE STEPS

Fig. 39.

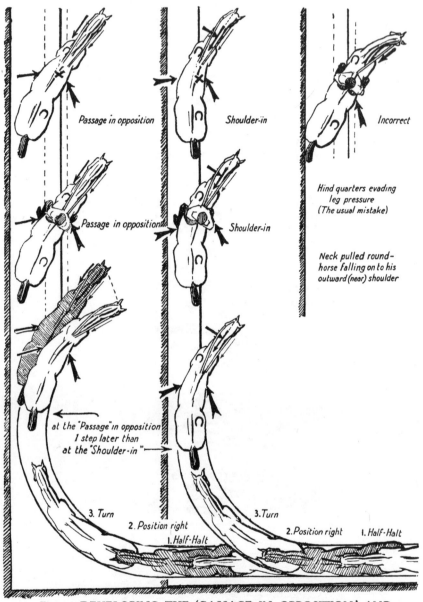

Fig. 40. DEVELOPING THE 'PASSAGE IN OPPOSITION' AND
'SHOULDER-IN' FROM A CORNER

opposite to the direction of movement. It is not particularly suited to increase the action of the haunches or to collect the horse. It is merely a means of increasing obedience to the inner leg and should only be ridden for a few steps.

Amongst the side movements we distinguish between 'shoulder in', 'passage' and 'counter passage'. The purpose of these movements is to complete the physical training of the

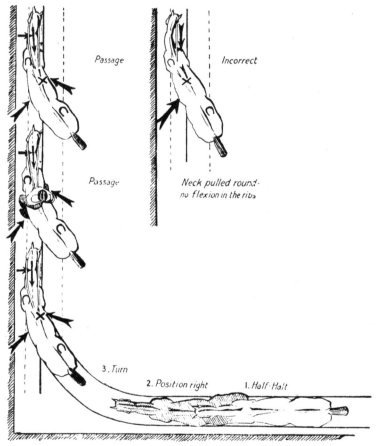

Fig. 41. DEVELOPING THE 'PASSAGE' (TRAVERS)
from a corner

horse and to increase flexion of the ribs. Side steps should only be attempted by riders with a very well established and confirmed seat and with years of practice and experience. They are not an end in itself, but a means only to the horse's education and to the obtaining of an increased degree of collection.

'Leg yielding' is a suppling exercise (and punishment). The legs step over and in front of each other, and definitely on two tracks.

In 'shoulder in' the inner hind leg follows the outer front leg and steps directly under the centre of gravity, being, therefore, a very good exercise for collecting the horse.

SHORT 'ABOUT-TURN'

This is a fluent 'pivot on the haunches' while the horse is in motion. It should, therefore, be tried by the rider only when he is absolutely certain that he can execute the pivot on the haunches at the halt.

The short about-turn is first practised at the walk, similarly to the way in which the pivot on the haunches was developed from the walk (see p. 130), simultaneously flexing the horse while pulling up to the halt, thus executing the first step of the pivot. The outer rein and outer leg press the horse round and flex him towards the inside, exactly as at the pivot; the inner leg prevents the horse from crawling back, but does not limit each single step as it formerly did in the pivot on the haunches at the standstill. The whole turn should be carried out fluently in one graceful movement.

In the short about-turn the horse walks, trots or canters round the inner hind leg.

For preliminary practice for the short about-turn the 'volte' can be used. It begins with a half-volte, after finishing which, the track is reached on an incline. With advanced education it is instructive for both rider and horse to make the volte with the outer leg 'narrowing the circle'. This is of special importance and very instructive in turns at the canter. Such a turn is the best preliminary lesson for the 'short about-turn at the canter'.

The endeavour to make short about-turns rapidly and fluently must not lead to the mistake of finishing them as quickly as possible by pulling at the reins ! The criterion of these turns is *not the speed* with which the horse throws himself round, but the *correctness of each single step*. Horses which are not well at the aids will always resent its execution and will indicate this by throwing their heads about, crawling backwards or even rearing.

IV

EXERCISES FOR THE FURTHER TRAINING OF RIDER AND HORSE

SOLO RIDING

RIDING INSTRUCTION is frequently given in classes, but it is often said that riding can only be taught in solo lessons. This is not quite correct, inasmuch as instruction in classes offers considerable advantages, apart from the fact that it is, of course, much cheaper. The great gain lies in the fact that it increases the ambition and zeal of each rider. For the instructor, again, it offers the opportunity of comparing the talent and proficiency of his various pupils at each stage of the education. Lastly, in instruction classes it is possible for the pupils to change horses very often, a procedure which is necessary for the development of 'feel'.

We talk of 'solo riding' if a rider works his horse alone and is not confined to a certain place in a class. He need not then adapt himself to the pace of the others, or keep at a certain distance, or execute a particular movement together with others. He can do anything when he thinks and feels that he has properly prepared for it.

In all courses of riding instructions, solo riding is used as a valuable part of the training. But it is only of use and to the advantage of the rider if he knows what he wants to practice. In most cases the instructor will indicate certain lines, but even if he does not, the young rider should know what he wants to do and should have a definite idea as to what lesson he proposes to practise.

Solo riding affords an opportunity of testing everything

connected with seat, feel and influence, all lessons and all aids. It is best to begin with the simplest and most elementary things: influence of the back-muscles, following the movement of the horse, walking on, halts and half-halts (see p. 113).

The feel for lateral aids and influences must be shaped by exercising the pivot on the haunches. In solo riding, it is important that this pivot be executed at any spot of the riding school, preferably in the middle. If the rider thinks that he has really mastered the pivot on the haunches at the halt he can gradually try to do it from the walk, and then go on to do the short about-turn (see p. 148).

Solo riding also affords the best opportunity of practising 'cantering on' (see p. 130), because in a class one cannot so frequently canter on and halt again. Practice of this cantering on is very important for developing the feel, educating the rider to stick like glue to the saddle and giving him an opportunity to feel if his horse leads on the proper leg. When no difficulties are experienced in cantering on, halting and cantering on again, the requirements can gradually be increased. Naturally, one should not *always* pull up after the third or fourth stride of the canter, or the horse will make a habit of it and finally stop of his own accord. One should let him go three strides at one time, eight at another, and five at a third, but in any case each time a different number of strides. It is well to count the strides in order to be perfectly certain that one does not gradually fall into easy mechanical ways. Cantering on should be exercised alternately on both hands, until precision and reliability of execution are attained.

Another very instructive lesson is the 'changing in the circle' at the canter. Shortly before reaching the centre of the circle there must be a decisive half-halt, then opposite flexion and cantering on again.

In order to make these exercises a little more complicated and also to refine feel and influences, one can alternately trot on from the walk, then canter on, then trot on again, then canter on again and so forth. This exercise can be so highly developed that on a single circle one can canter on four times and trot on four times from the walk, and the same can be practised in riding on a straight line, cantering on alternately with the right leg or the left leg leading.

One should make it a rule in solo riding never to ride more than half a school without interrupting the monotony by a half-halt or halt or other change of pace or by some figure. When one can think of nothing else to ride, it is best to go over to a walk with long reins and take a rest, but one should never allow oneself to be sloppily carried about without a definite plan.

It is possible to practise entirely different types of exercises: one can ride away from the class with a message, ride between two objects, do a lateral exercise or some jumping; or one can use the opportunity to have special things explained by the instructor. Then, one can ask to be put on another horse, especially one whose bad habits one thinks one has recognized and which one would like to experience. The great axioms for all these lessons, however, are: that it is never a question of which exercise is to be practised, but 'how' it is practised. And every lesson must be well thought over before doing it, and finally every lesson should at first be made as simple and as easy as possible for both man and mount.

SHOW RIDING

It is often said of show riding that it spoils a horseman's character, because riding of this kind is no longer an end in itself, but is overshadowed by ambition and the spirit of competition. On the other hand, the preparations for a show or tournament are very valuable because the powerful incentive of ambition urges a man to almost inconceivable accomplishments, perseverance, thoroughness and conscientiousness.

At a test or trial the rider should always keep strictly to the prescribed figures, otherwise neither judges nor spectators will be able to recognize whether he is actually in position to lead his horse in the correct way. The closer the rider sticks to the figures, the more will everybody get the impression that he has genuine control over his horse. For instance, 'changing in the circle' and the 'figure 8 at the canter', with change of lead at the centre of the circle, at a right angle to the short wall of the school, is one of the severest and most exacting tests. The young rider who has not frequently practised these lessons and who has not tried them over and over again will certainly not be able to do them. He will hardly know where the real difficulties lie and how tactfully the horse must be managed in order to ride the correct line. The most common mistakes are, that the first half-circle is usually made too wide, that the rider thinks too late of the half-halt and consequently does not come vertically towards the short wall, and that instead of finishing the eight at the spot where he started, he ends up miles away. If the horse is to change the leading leg at the centre of the figure 8, he must be pulled up by a half-halt at least two to three yards before reaching this point, so that he can be flexed quietly and unhurriedly to the other side before cantering on again. It is well to try these figures first at the walk. In the first few trials at the canter the half-halt should be made at least ten to fifteen yards before arriving at the centre, and the rider should take all his time for cantering on on the other hand.

Voltes and about-turns which are not executed exactly in the corners of the school will always induce a certain amount of indecision in the young rider. He will not know how to execute these turns, where to begin and where to end them. And as soon as he loses decision, the movements of his horse will promptly betray the fact. In show riding, also, the various paces at the walk, trot and canter must be absolutely clear and well defined; the horse must never go 'just a trot', or 'just a canter'. It must always be either a 'collected trot', a 'middle

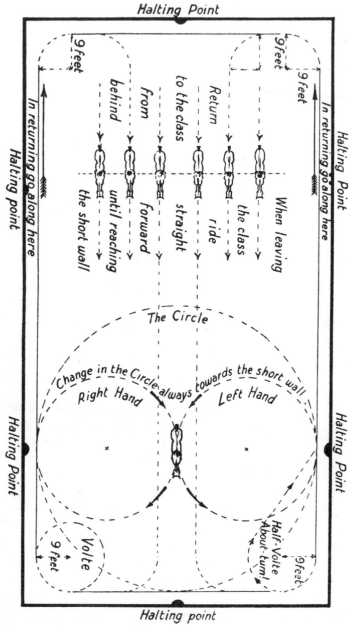

Fig. 42. CORRECT MANEGE FIGURES

Halting Point

Halting Point

Halting Point

Halting point

Halting Point

Halting point

In returning go along here

In returning go along here

9 feet

9 feet

9 feet

When leaving

Return ride

to the class

straight

From forward

behind until reaching

the short wall

The Circle

Change in the Circle always towards the short wall

Right Hand

Left Hand

Half-Volte
About-turn!

Volte

9 feet

9 feet

trot', or an 'extended trot', and the differences between these paces (and the corresponding paces at the other gaits) must be absolutely distinct and clear.

RIDING ACROSS COUNTRY

Riding is a matter of practice, and the more pleasure a person finds on horseback, the more will his ambition be aroused, and the more intensely will he occupy himself with the art ! There is, therefore, hardly a better aid to the furtherance of the education of a rider than riding across country !

'Any country looks twice as nice when seen between the ears of a horse.'

A long ride across country, even if there is no instruction at all, will improve the rider's seat, because he will more readily relax. He is sure to sit better, much better than when trying to force himself into a so-called 'correct' position. Once he is feeling comfortable on horseback, which he will do after a number of long rides, he will no longer make himself stiff and rigid whenever he is being corrected or given instructive advice.

All training is therefore greatly helped by riding across country, much more so than is generally assumed. It is *not* a waste of time, as is often contended by the guild of school riders. A long quiet canter and a long quiet trot often do wonders, and those riders who in riding across country detect their shortcomings on the one or the other occasion, and see that they are helpless now and then, will always ask their instructor to show them this or that, explain this thing or the other, and they will follow the lessons in the riding school with much more interest and ambition.

Riding across country must constantly, and at all times, be practised as a substantial part of the training. The rider who believes he has his horse under perfect control in the school should make the test and see whether he has not been deceived by the quiet seclusion of the covered school. Riding across country quickly brings to light whether the rider has really learned 'to ride' and whether he really sits comfortably, or whether he has just been forced into a form which may, perhaps, be pleasant to the eye. There, too, it will soon be apparent whether the horse has really and genuinely been 'put to the aids', whether he pays attention to the rider or whether the most important point of all has been overlooked or neglected for the sake of a pleasant appearance ! Riding in the open, across country, is the best and most convincing test of all dressage !

The sad experiences, however, which cross-country riding often produces with so-called 'schooled' horses should not induce the intelligent rider to condemn the system of 'dressage'. Certainly many horses which are always being ridden across country will *appear* to go much better, will seem quieter and less apt to shy, than 'dressage' horses which have been ridden continually in a school. But that, of course, is the merest fallacy ! If the dressage has been carried out correctly the horse must give a more comfortable and agreeable ride. He must go anywhere at any time—with a minimum of exertion for the rider and himself and a maximum of comfort and reliability. Riding across country, after all, is not only just a test, it is the ultimate goal of all training—including dressage ! Therefore, the cardinal point in dressage-work is that the horse should not only 'appear' to be 'at the aids' and obedient, but that he should really be under complete and absolute control. And to develop the feel for this is the foremost task in the training of the rider.

POSTING

Posting, as against 'sitting down' in the saddle, makes things easier for both rider and horse. For this reason, it is always used in riding across country. In school riding posting is used much less, because the contact between the rider's buttocks and the saddle lasts only a few moments at each stride and the rider has therefore less time to 'feel by his seat'. For purposes of moving a horse (working trot, loosening up) and at the extended trot, posting is also used in the covered school.

When posting, the rider finds his support in the stirrups and rises when a diagonal pair of legs leave the ground. He lowers himself again into the saddle in the following stage and rises again immediately. He always touches the saddle simultaneously with the placing of the right or the left hind leg on the ground. This is called 'posting on the right or the left hind leg'. In the school the rider should always post on the inner hind leg. In a change of hand, he should therefore change the leg on which he posts. He should also be careful when going across country from time to time to change the foot on which he posts in order not to overstrain one or other foot. If the rider does not pay attention to this he will most certainly find himself posting on one particular foot all the time. This is due to the unequal development of the two sides of a horse. There is always a 'smooth and a bumpy' side. When posting, the driving influences of back and legs must be exerted in the same manner as in the 'German trot', or sitting down in the saddle. It is wrong if the rider, in posting, leans too far forward, believing that he can dispense with back influences.

RIDING UP-HILL AND DOWN-HILL

Owing to their natural timidity all horses go very cautiously over uneven ground and therefore are quite safe if they are not interfered with. They are more clever in going down-hill than up-hill. Down-hill they can manage much steeper slopes than up-hill. Horses invariably *walk* down-hill. If the angle is more than fifty degrees they ultimately sit down on their haunches and slide.

In riding down-hill it is important for the rider to overlook the ground so that he can pick the 'line' he wants to ride and not, so to speak, go blindfold into the uncertain. He must sit

Fig. 43. GOING DOWN-HILL

well forward, resting his hands on the withers, being careful not to slide on to the neck. In this manner the rider is able to direct his horse; he can avoid stones, roots, or slippery spots, pick the best line down-hill, and thus negotiate quite amazingly steep hills. There is not the slightest difficulty at this seat to maintain contact with the horse's body and, by leg action, to prevent the hind quarters from moving sideways—the gravest danger in going down very steep slopes. If, on slippery ground or wet grass, or very soft sand or on rocks, the haunches slip sideways, the horse cannot save himself and must inevitably turn turtle.

If the rider leans backward he can neither keep contact by his legs with the horse's body, nor avoid slipping forward in the saddle. Also, he has no chance to overlook the ground in front of him. This type of seat is completely wrong; it is unsafe and dangerous !

Much has been said and written about the theory of the distribution of weight in riding down-hill and about the 'heavier load on the front legs or the hind legs' caused by the weight of the rider. All these theoretical discussions are useless and mostly miss the point, as is apparent from the figure on this page.

In riding up-hill the greatest danger lies in being 'left behind'. The rider tries to hang on to the mouth, checking the horse's eager attempts to go forward and to climb. The

steeper the slope the more
anxious will the horse be to
rush it, to take it at a canter
or in gallop-like strides.

The rider who wants to
maintain contact between his
hands and the horse's mouth
will (as also most probably in
jumping) pull too much at
the reins and hold his horse
back. It is therefore better
and of greater advantage to
give up all contact with the
mouth, and, on very steep
hills, to 'take the horse round
the neck'. Mouth and neck
will then be entirely free and
unhampered, the horse can
choose his own pace, and it is

Fig. 44. GOING UP-HILL

only necessary to shift one's centre of gravity forward as much
as possible in order not to be left behind. The horse, with a
free neck, will pick the best line for himself, and it is not at all
difficult to give a little help with direction. The loss of contact
between the rider's hands and the horse's mouth is of no grave
consequence, for, as in jumping, the contact should in any case
have been no more than trifling. It does not make much
difference to the horse if this contact is suddenly given up: he
will just make his neck longer and use it as his natural balancing
pole. And that is what we want him to do.

JUMPING

Although the principles of dressage have changed comparatively little since the time of Xenophon, the ideas and theories
on jumping are of comparatively recent date. Jumping for

jumping's sake, as this rather popular sport exists to-day, was hardly known until shortly before the war or perhaps the beginning of this century. True, hunting dates back several centuries, especially in France and England, but the jumping of obstacles was not an end in itself. It was never really investigated; there was never any 'research work' carried on; and the views of jumping in those times no longer bear close scrutiny.

The modern art of jumping originated in Italy. The modern jumping style is therefore usually called 'Italian'. In jumping, much more than in dressage or any other work, the rider must depend on the goodwill and ability of his horse. And every rider should above all keep well in mind that the horse will jump an obstacle well and properly only if he wants to!

The high jump record for

Man is approximately	6ft. 8ins.
Horse with rider	7ft. 10ins.
The average gymnast jumps . . .	4ft. 4ins.
The untrained cow in the paddock jumps	4ft.

Should not a horse easily jump 4ft. 8ins? If he does not, we can be certain that we have not understood how to make him like it!

Jumping and dressage, however, are not, as is often wrongly assumed, antithetical and exclusive of each other. The better a horse responds to the aids the more willingly will he go over jumps.

SCHOOLING THE HORSE OVER JUMPS

This training comprises:
(1) Getting the horse to like jumping.
(2) Training, i.e. developing the muscles and
(3) The routine of approach.

The correct development in these three respects requires just as painstaking a study of the horse's psychology as dressage.

To the uninitiated spectator, a good jumping rider may often appear to work all his horses after one pattern. Yet amongst 'jumpers' there are ambitious and lazy ones, 'hot ones' and sluggish ones, timid and courageous souls; one horse responds more to patting and fondling, another to punishment. Some horses have more love and aptitude for jumping than others, and will therefore pick it up quicker than their brethren.

A horse's memory plays a decisive part in jumping. A horse never quite forgets a mishap or a certain obstacle at which he fell or hurt himself. It will largely depend on his character whether, after such a mishap, he is more careful the next time and pulls up his legs a little closer to the body or whether he loses his nerve altogether.

In schooling a horse over jumps, it is essential to observe the most seemingly unimportant little details. In jumping, 'education' is all and everything, and one cannot possibly over-rate its importance.

There are various ways in which a horse can be trained over jumps; the actual height of the obstacles makes little difference. Training a horse to jump a course of three feet obstacles in good style wants just as much study and care as the training of a high-jumper. The only difference is that mistakes in handling will be noticeable sooner with greater height, but they can be made just as easily over jumps of two feet and can have the same fatal consequences.

Horses can be jumped-in with or without a rider. As a rule both methods are used in combination. Without a rider the horse can either be led close up to the obstacle, or he can be jumped on the lunge or 'in liberty' in a special jumping paddock. Sometimes the horse is made to jump one obstacle at a time, sometimes several in succession. This can be done either in the covered school or in an open paddock. The paddock can either be an oblong rectangle, straight (jumping lane), or round (couloir). The horse can be asked to jump several obstacles with shorter or longer spaces in between. It is impossible to

II

give a general prescription or 'recipe', because these things must be adapted to the degree of training to be aimed at and to the character of the animal. The main object of all the exercises must be to increase the horse's 'love for the *métier*', and to teach him to use proper judgement in the approach and the take off. To work after a set scheme only results in disaster. And under the rider the procedure must be varied and adapted to the horse in a like manner. By combining the two, jumping without the rider and jumping under the rider, monotony is taken out of the training. One can jump a horse for days and weeks without a rider and then for weeks again with a rider, or vice versa. All these questions are, of course, dictated to a certain extent by the prevailing circumstances and available facilities. In town it may be necessary to remain more often in the school, whereas in the country one can probably jump more in the open. The greater the understanding of the character of the horse the sooner we can make him jump all kinds of obstacles. However, if jumping-in is done without a lot of care and study and if one tries to treat all horses alike, one cannot expect good results.

THE APPROACH

The most common mistake made in jumping is neglect of the approach. The execution of a jump is once and for all determined by the take off. There is an old adage: 'Throw your heart over and jump after it !' The feelings and sensations of the rider are naturally communicated to the horse through his influences, their emphasis, their determination or indetermination. The horse therefore feels very definitely whether his rider is determined to jump or whether he is timid and approaches the obstacle a little shakily. He will only jump willingly and with decision if he is 'put' absolutely 'straight at it'. Otherwise he gets startled and falters, and, especially if he is unconsciously held back by the reins, will refuse to jump.

For ordinary jumping purposes the leathers should be made

one to two holes shorter. The best pace for approaching an obstacle is the canter, because that is the most comfortable one for the horse. It is possible to jump from the walk or the trot, but the natural pace is the canter, because the cadence of the jump is the same as that of the canter. In jumping from the trot or the walk the horse is obliged to change the sequence of the foot-fall at the last moment. In the paddock we should always jump from the canter of the particular hand on which we are riding. There are horses, however, who often change before the take-off, preferring always to jump from a certain leg. Over low fences it usually makes no difference to most horses.

The pace of the last few strides of the approach is regulated by the horse.

An athlete who is about to jump will certainly not let anybody interfere with his approach or determine his pace. He could not possibly jump as well and as safely as if his approach had not been interfered with. Every rider should bear this well in mind ! One horse will prefer to jump from a slower pace, stretching his neck as if he wanted to have a last good sniff at the obstacle before jumping. Another will 'get up more steam', moving faster and faster the nearer he gets to the fence. These different ways of approaching an obstacle are more or less habits which horses acquire during their first schooling over jumps. It is quite possible that in both the instances given above the horse would jump better if he went about it the other way round; but that cannot be decided in a hurry and cannot easily be corrected. And certainly not by a rider who has not had a lot of experience himself.

With increased experience, routine and practice, a horse will automatically correct his approach. Old, experienced horses negotiate high jumps invariably at a collected canter and long jumps (wide ditches) at a faster pace. Less experienced horses, of course, hardly know the difference.

It is wrong to indicate to the horse when he should take off—

by pulling at the reins or 'giving him the office' as it is commonly termed, or by raising the hands or by a tap of the whip or by the voice. Highly experienced riders can sometimes, for certain reasons, come to such an agreement with a horse; but these are rare exceptions. By shouting 'hop' inexperienced riders in most cases do nothing but encourage themselves! The use of the whip requires enormous practice. It is almost impossible not to disturb the horse with it by changing one's seat. 'Following the movement' of the horse in jumping is quite an undertaking in itself and there are indeed extremely few people who can, at the same time, keep the left hand with the reins perfectly still and swing the right arm with the whip.

If a horse runs out in front of an obstacle he can have many reasons for doing it. He can have been influenced by an undetermined approach on the part of the rider or by a clumsy movement with reins, legs, weight, or whip. It can also be caused by the nature of the soil, which may be too slippery or too heavy; or the appearance of the particular obstacle may have startled him. He can also have been irritated by some noise or by other horses in the vicinity. Another reason may be that the horse has not properly learned to jump or that he just does not want to jump that particular obstacle because he has hurt himself at it on a previous occasion.

The reason for the disobedience must be investigated. It is impossible to enumerate all the various reasons for a horse running out, and as the remedy must always depend on the nature of the cause of the trouble, it is impossible to give a general recipe in the limited space of this book. Sometimes it would perhaps be well to tidy the approach in front of the obstacle or the obstacle itself or to adjust saddle and tackle. Sometimes it is better to forget the whip and instead ride forward with determination; in many cases the desired result will be brought about by just turning and 'riding at it' again. Sometimes a few steps 'reining back' will be of advantage. If an obstacle requires a long run (the necessity of a long run is mostly over-valued) one should first rein back a few steps and then make an about-turn. If an instructor is present he will be able to give the proper advice, but it is in very bad form and poor taste to 'fight it out' with a 'hireling', especially if one does not know how the thing is done and cannot, from sheer lack of knowledge and experience, determine the cause of the refusal.

If a horse refuses at the second attempt the proper thing to do is to quit, unless the instructor or some other experienced jumping rider is near by to help. In the first place, however, one should remain quiet on the refusing horse and not fall into a blind rage, jabbing and stabbing at the poor animal, who is probably not to be blamed at all. Even the most expert athlete will sometimes make a blunder in approaching a jump, but his comrades do not dash at him and 'knock him to pieces !'

BEHAVIOUR DURING THE JUMP

In discussing jumping, most people think of nothing but the rider's seat while in the air. Yet it cannot be said often enough that the rider's behaviour during the jump proper is by no means as decisive as is generally assumed, although it is, of course, important to some extent. The schooling of the horse over jumps and—at a later stage—the approach (discussed in the last two chapters) are at least as important as the rider's behaviour during the jump. On a well-schooled jumper even the poorest beginner will probably make a tolerable figure. But, of course, if a well-schooled horse is constantly annoyed by the rider and put at the obstacle without energy, he will soon lose all taste for jumping, no matter how good he may have been ! Photographs give sufficient proof that some of the most successful jumping riders do not always sit—theoretically —correctly, and yet their horses jump willingly and safely. On the other hand, the most beautiful style will not help much if the rider has no nerve and does not know how to approach a jump.

There is still a good deal of difference between the various

views on the technique of jumping. This may be partly due
to the fact that one section of jumping riders sees the whole
thing only from a practical point of view, while the other section would like to answer all questions in a more theoretical
manner, according to the principles of dressage. In practice,
the Italian seat has absolutely conquered the field. Yet
opinions differ as to what the Italian seat actually is and what
are its greatest merits. We talk of 'freeing the haunches', of
the necessary 'going with the horse', yet we require, on the
other hand, that the rider keep as near to the saddle as possible,

Fig. 10. THE JUGGLER

and that his hands maintain a certain contact with the horse's
mouth.

We say that balance and harmony between rider and horse
are established if there is co-ordination of their respective
centres of gravity. Let us study the picture of a horse jumping
at liberty, and at the same time recall the juggler's balancing
act.

In the first phase of the jump, immediately after the take-
off, the rider's behaviour is decisively influenced by:

(*a*) the sudden acceleration,

(*b*) the change of direction upwards.

Since, in jumping from the walk or from the trot, acceleration is greater than in jumping from the canter, the latter is, as previously said, not only easier for the horse, but also for the rider.

The higher the jump the more will the upward change of direction influence the rider's seat.   Over high jumps, however, this does not depend absolutely on the height of the obstacle but more on the distance from it at which the horse takes off.

If the rider wants to remain in harmony with his horse he must bring his centre of gravity *ahead of* that of the horse; he

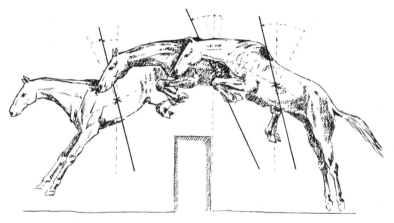

Fig. 45. HORSE JUMPING IN LIBERTY

must lean forward, towards the horse's neck; and it follows that over a high jump he cannot keep his buttocks in the saddle. The slower the pace at which he approaches the obstacle the less will he be able to remain 'seated' at the take-off.

In the second phase of the jump the horse no longer moves upward but merely forward, horizontally across the obstacle. Although the rider's centre of gravity should continue to be in front of the horse's, it will now be much more nearly perpendicular to the horse's back than before.   In this phase, therefore, the rider could bring his buttocks closer to the saddle.

Fig. 46. GOOD

THE SEAT

*The dotted lines connect the centres of gravity of horse and rider and by their inclina-
tion indicate the degree by which the rider has to lean himself 'into the movement'.
This cannot be seen by the mere leaning forward of the body*

In the third phase, before landing, the rider's centre of
gravity would still be in front of the horse's, even if he sat at a
right angle to the horse's back, and his buttocks could therefore now be in the saddle.

During the approach a rider can never tell how his horse is
going to jump. Consequently he must always be prepared to
lift his seat, and must learn by practice the feel for how much
or how far he must shift his centre of gravity in any particular
case. The study of action photographs can here be of great
help and the essential question of the 'relative position of the
two centres of gravity' should be constantly borne in mind.
But beware of harmful deceptions! A forward inclination of
the upper part of the body does not necessarily mean a displacement of the centre of gravity towards the front! It is quite
possible that, in 'leaning forward', the rider may move his

Exaggeration   *Behind the movement*

Fig. 47. BAD

OVER A JUMP

No leaning forward, no stretching of the arms can prevent the rider from being left behind once he has missed at the rise his opportunity to follow the movement

centre of gravity to the rear.   If, for instance, the buttocks are pushed back beyond the cantle, the rider is then sitting as if on a motor-cycle.   This mistake often occurs.   As soon as the rider has grasped the essentials of the 'jumping seat', the problem of whether his buttocks should be down in the saddle or not, will be solved quite automatically.   If the centre of gravity *can* be shifted towards the front while the buttocks remain in the saddle, they *should* remain there.   If it is necessary to shift the centre of gravity further forward, this will not allow of the buttocks remaining in the saddle, and they *must* be lifted out of it.

It is therefore clear that, for the jumping seat, the rider requires a different 'fixed purchase' from the usual.   This difference is so decisive that it cannot be expressed too clearly and too strongly.

The new basis consists in the first place of 'knee grip'.   The knees must be pressed firmly against the horse's body and must remain there as if they were screwed on to it. Even if one of the leathers should break, the rider ought not immediately to lose his balance.

For this reason the leathers are shortened, in order to raise the knees in the saddle and facilitate a strong grip; the feet are thrust well home in the stirrups, *but the heels must not be raised*. The lower legs always maintain their position close behind the girth. It is utterly wrong to put them further back or to stretch them away, both of which would only irritate the horse.

During the jump the hands rest on the horse's neck or take hold of the mane. The arms remain bent at the elbow, so that the rider can at any moment 'give' a whole arm's length, should that be necessary.

The horse begins to rise to the jump out of the third phase of the gallop (see Figs. on p. 135), in which he pushes himself off the ground with his fore legs and then catapults himself upward by means of the hind legs, which, to this end, are tucked well under the body. This moment is the beginning of the rise and the latest instant at which the rider can determinedly bring his centre of gravity forward. The earlier he has made preparation for this the easier it will be for him at the moment of the rise.

If one is forced to urge and drive a horse towards an obstacle, it will only be possible to give up contact with the saddle shortly before the take-off, for the driving influence of the back and legs cease as soon as the rider's buttocks leave the saddle. Thus it can even happen with the very best riders that in such cases (when they have to 'ride him' close up to the obstacle) they miss the proper time for shifting their centre of gravity and are then 'left behind'. If this moment has been missed, no stretching of the arms or leaning forward in the saddle will help. Such movements, inevitable though they are, always look like gross exaggerations, which actually they are not at all. But they not only look unharmonious, they also show clearly that harmony has been destroyed and that the rider is not balanced. If, on such occasions, the rider does not sufficiently grip with his knees and lower legs the horse will probably jump from under him. When thus 'left behind' the rider should at least try not to hinder the horse still more by pulling at the reins or reward his loyal services with the usual solid bump in the back.

Well-jumped-in horses will 'draw towards the obstacle'. On such horses the rider can assume the jumping seat much earlier. If a horse is sufficiently willing to go, and if several jumps have to be taken in succession, it is better to maintain this seat during the whole course. Driving or urging the horse is then done exclusively with the lower legs.

The rider's hands during the jump are low. They either rest on the neck or grip the horse's mane; in any case the rider has contact with the horse's neck which otherwise he has not. He can, if he is very clever, maintain a certain contact with the horse's mouth; but as this contact should always be a light one, being, in fact, only a few ounces, it will probably not matter at all if it is lost at the moment of the take-off, that is, if the reins hang loosely. It would be quite wrong to require an appreciable contact with the horse's mouth, if it involves the danger of bothering the horse by a jerk at the reins. The rider should always bear in mind this most important thing: *the horse must be given sufficient freedom to stretch his neck.* Not only will he jump much more willingly, but the leap is much safer with a long, outstretched neck. If the rider feels during the jump a heavier contact on the reins than he felt before, it follows that he has made a mistake; and if the horse does not jump with a long, stretched neck the same mistake must have been made.

The young rider will best learn the jumping seat on a well-schooled horse, without reins, by holding on to the mane or to a strap round the horse's neck (breastplate). It is a grave mistake to hold on to the saddle because this does not obviate being 'left behind', and it does make it impossible to 'follow the movement'. Once the rider has acquired the feel for following the movement, he will very soon arrive at the stage where he can do it by merely resting his hands on the neck without having to hold on to the mane or to a strap. It is then that the young rider should test his knee-grip by jumping without stirrups. Jumping with crossed arms or with hands resting on the hips and similar tricks are absolutely useless; the rider learns nothing from them, and is constantly left behind.

MISTAKES OF THE HORSE IN JUMPING

Even the very best 'lepper' can sometimes make one of the following mistakes:

(1) Run up too close to the obstacle, and have to jump very steeply.

(2) Take-off too soon, thereby being forced to 'stretch' across the obstacle.

(3) Misjudge the height, with the result that the hind quarters have to be thrown over sideways to avoid a knock.

At such moments the rider must be able to help the horse by giving him all the freedom he wants. For this reason the arms should normally be bent at the elbows to allow of a good range of stretch. The horse can balance and compensate with his neck all the movements mentioned before. And if at the critical moment (a matter of only a fraction of a second) he cannot stretch as much as he wants to, he will certainly make a much bigger mistake, a mistake which, in certain circumstances, can be fatal.

There is no necessity for any contact with the horse's mouth during the jump proper, and after the jump it is quite automatically re-established.

THE PECK

In landing likewise this contact is not necessary, not even if the horse makes a blunder. In this case the contact, even should it be only a few ounces too heavy, can only have deplorable consequences ! A great many falls are the result of a peck, very often only because the rider thinks he must help the horse by 'pulling him up'. The inexperienced beginner thinks to lift the horse in front of him by a pull at the reins, but at the same time he inevitably presses him down at the rear. By a jerk at the mouth, or by too heavy a contact, many a rider has robbed his horse of the last chance of recovery. A stumbling rope dancer inevitably falls if, at the critical moment, his balancing pole catches in something. The horse can only recover from a peck by balancing himself with neck and head.

The rider cannot do better than remain immovable, sitting as quietly and as tightly as possible; a shifting of his centre of gravity, which would throw the horse over, is as good as useless. After all, the rider has a certain weight (being no balloon with appropriate lifting power) and should naturally therefore be as closely connected with his horse as possible. The rider who has the firmest seat has the greatest chance to recover from a peck.

It is wrong to conclude from the heavier contact with the mouth felt during a peck, that the horse has perhaps tried to establish this contact and that it helps him. Would not a falling man pull and tear at the ropes if his hands were tied ?

LANDING

In landing, the rider's knees act, so to speak, as shock absorbers; they are elastic joints and consequently quite comfortable for the horse, with whose body they are not rigidly connected, being only pressed sideways to it by the rider's muscles. Likewise the arms, which find a purchase in the hands on the neck, act somehow as spring joints at elbows and shoulders. Therefore, landing is, without doubt, more comfortable for the horse when he is ridden with the Italian seat than when the rider leans his body backwards and the full impact of his weight bears down on the saddle from top to bottom, or rather from rear to front.

After the jump the rider must as quickly as possible re-establish full control over the horse. With the completion of the jump the rider's will must again be in the ascendant, resolving either to ride straight ahead or to turn or to approach a new obstacle. Consequently, the rider must as quickly as possible take up the reins and reseat himself in the saddle.

HUNTING

No other branch of riding arouses more enthusiasm for its beauty than hunting. No horseman who ever rode to a good pack ever forgets this pleasure all his life. In a hunt the rider is at his goal. In a good fast run across fields and through dales, over hills and ditches, over walls, gates, and fences, it will come home to the rider why, and to what end, he has worked hard for years in the riding school. Hunting was, from of old, the aristocrat of all sports, and through centuries has retained its exclusive character. As there are no competitions and no 'records', there are no endeavours to secure advantages, no mean petty jealousy. It is, in the true sense of the word, the sport of a gentleman. It requires nerve and courage, control of the horse, and—last but not least, for it is to the benefit of horse breeding—it wants a good hunter !

It is not exactly necessary for a hunter to please the eyes of judges in the show ring or that he be particularly young or good looking. A hunt is really a test of stamina. Across country a horse must be safe; he must not refuse a ditch or a fence; he must not stumble or be lazy; and it is also important and perhaps imperative that he should not hang heavy on the bit. In a hunt any horse will go better than usual. Many a horse that is otherwise sluggish and lazy will suddenly wake up in company and can hardly be 'held'; but to be stampeded along on a mad puller, is no pleasure. It is a danger to the rider himself as well as to all the followers of the hunt. The choice of a hunter wants a lot of experience and young riders should by all means seek the advice of seasoned experts at the game.

As long as a rider has no practice in 'riding to hounds' and has not the necessary knowledge, which can only be the product of experience, he will not have an opportunity to 'ride' his horse properly by his influences and 'half-halts'; he will more or less try to 'steer' somehow. The quieter the horse the sooner will the rider be able to stay the pace of a hunt.

Before the hunt starts, one should always see that saddle and bridle are well in order and that bandages are tight and secure. The stirrups are better shortened by two holes. Experienced riders assume during the whole hunt a modified jumping seat; they do not find their purchase in the buttocks, but rather in knees and stirrups. This type of seat is much less tiresome, especially in a long hunt. At a long, fast gallop it is difficult and tiring to sit down in the saddle; it often leads to the rider 'being behind the movement' and hanging on to the reins, not only over the jumps, but also at the canter and gallop.

If a horse refuses a jump the rider should exercise consideration for others and not block the obstacle by repeated turns and attempts to force his horse over. If he can, he will be well advised to hang on to another rider, but he should never jump in line behind his man, but always a little to the side. If your horse, however, cannot be 'lured' over the obstacle by a leader (following his gregarious instinct) it is better to find some other way of following the field than trying to 'fight it out'. It is rather depressing to a beginner to be left far behind and to finish the hunt hours after the kill. But a little patience and experience will soon show him that this can happen even to the most experienced riders ! The better the horse the easier it is to ride a hunt. There is no special merit in jumping an obstacle at the highest or widest spot, or in surmounting particularly difficult places. One should always, if possible, try to find the easiest going, for this reason: that one should always keep one's eyes wide open to the front. One should arrive at·the kill with as fresh a horse as possible!

If the rider loses control over his horse he must try somehow to get away from the field, in order not to molest others or to over-ride hounds (see p. 111 for handling a bolting horse).

No horseman who is lucky enough to have an opportunity of taking part in a hunt should ever miss it! The main conditions, however, are a suitable hunter, a fair amount of safety in the saddle, and nerve. Each and every hunt should be a festive occasion in a rider's life!

V

RIDING TACKLE

BRIDLES

EVERYTHING CONCERNING BRIDLES AND SADDLES should be explained by the instructor at the end of each riding lesson. The rider himself should inspect his own bridle and saddle before mounting.

Fig. 48.

If curb reins are slightly taut:
  A. *Too severe*
  B. *Correct position*
  C. *Too slack*

The bridle must fit the horse's head. It must be neither too loose nor so tight that the bit hurts the horse's mouth by pulling it up too high at the corners. The throat-lash should be just loose enough to admit the flat fingers of the hand. A badly-fitted bridle which causes pain has considerable effect in the willingness of the horse.

The thicker the snaffle the softer it is. The more sensitive the horse is in the mouth the thicker should be the snaffle.

The curb must be broad enough for the horse's mouth. There are wide and narrow mouths. The finer the head of a horse (as with thoroughbreds or Arabs) the narrower must be the mouth-piece of the curb-bit; the larger the head the wider the mouth and the wider, of course, the bit. The more sensitive the horse is in the mouth the shorter must be the cheeks of the curb. The curb is a lever which acts the more strongly the greater the difference between the length of upper and lower parts of the cheeks (with loose reins the cheeks of the curb must be parallel with the horse's mouth). Between curb-chain and jaw there must be room enough to admit two fingers comfortably. In taking up the curb-reins the cheeks are turned by about thirty degrees. If it is possible to turn them more the curb-chain is too long, but if they cannot be turned that far, the curb-chain is too short.

SADDLES

The rider can only sit correctly and influence correctly if the saddle fits the horse. The lowest point of the saddle should be in the middle. If it is more to the rear or more to the front the rider is made to assume a wrong seat. A wrong position of the lowest point can have its cause in the tree being too wide for the horse's back or too narrow, or it can also be that the padding of the saddle is too thick or too thin. A saddle must fit a horse's back as closely as a suit fits a man. (See p. 99, the first horse in Fig. 24.)

BANDAGES

Bandages are to preserve the tendons. Their value is often over-rated. It sometimes happens that horses hurt themselves with their own shoes, knocking their legs, especially in quick turns or in stumbling, or when jumping. This can lead to splints (swellings in the bone), which can easily cause lameness. In general, bandages are a protection against knocks and bruises and a certain safeguard against sprains. To put on a bandage correctly requires a lot of practice. Special care must be taken that there are no creases. A badly-wrapped bandage can cause a 'leg' (soreness in the tendons). The ends of the bandage should be tied in a knot on the outside of the leg; they must not press against the leg where they can easily cause injuries. The knot should never lie on top of the tendon and must be tied sufficiently securely to prevent it coming undone during a ride. If a bandage gets undone the horse can easily take a nasty 'header'.

AUXILIARY REINS

We distinguish between the following auxiliary reins:

(1) Side reins. These are put on both sides of the horse, forming a connexion between the rings of the snaffle bit and the girth. The side reins are called 'short' if the horse takes his nose behind the perpendicular, so that his mouth comes nearer to the chest. They are called 'long' if the nose can be kept just in front of the perpendicular. For dressage purposes side reins should never be used because they always remain rigid in their action. They only serve for riding instruction with a beginner who has not yet learned to balance.

(2) The running martingale is a strap one end of which either forms a loop through which the girth passes or is buckled on to the breastplate. The two other (forked) ends carry rings through which the snaffle reins are drawn. The martingale must be long enough to hang loosely when the snaffle reins are stretched taut. If the horse tries to throw his head about or wants to poke it up in the air, the martingale cannot certainly prevent him from doing so, but it should to some extent limit the movement. Thus, the rider will not, at such moments, lose all control over his horse, and the martingale will prevent the horse's head hitting his face.

The photograph of Major Ricci (see Plate 13) shows a running martingale of correct length. The martingale is not a dressage tackle. It is particularly useful for jumping and hunting and, in general, for cross-country purposes, especially with 'hot' or fussy horses.[1]

(3) The Sliding Rein. This consists of two lengths of strap of approximately nine feet each. One end of the straps is buckled to the girth about as high as the rider's knee. The straps then pass through the rings of the snaffle (from inside to outside) and from there into the rider's hands, the left- or near-side rein into the left hand, the right- or off-side into the right hand. To avoid too much friction at the snaffle rings the smooth side of the leather should slide in the rings. (See Fig. 21, p. 81.)

The use of the sliding rein involves a danger, inasmuch as there is a tendency to pull the horse's mouth towards the chest unless they are handled very carefully. Sliding reins should only be used by riders who have a definite knowledge of what a horse should feel like when it is properly put to the aids and who thus knows how the horse's mouth can be pushed forward, as it were, by two rods. The sliding reins easily tempt the trainer to bring 'bridling' about by the mere action of the hands, without the horse being properly driven into the bridle, from rear to front, i.e. with 'collection'.

[1] Besides the running martingale there are the 'standing martingale' and the 'Irish martingale'. The former connects the girth with the noseband of the bridle, and must be sufficiently long to allow the horse to extend his neck sufficiently while jumping. The 'Irish martingale' is a short strap with a ring at each end through which the reins are drawn. It has no other purpose than to prevent both reins getting on one side of the neck if the horse, in a 'tussle' or at some fussy occasion, throws his head up high. THE TRANSLATOR.

Sliding reins must only be used in conjunction with adequate driving influences, and then only for short periods, as long as the horse shows a tendency to stiffen at the poll or in the jaws. A slight pressure on the inner sliding-rein—while simultaneously feeling forward with the outer—will probably induce the horse to give. This method of making a horse extend himself towards the ground has been fully described on p. 81. Sliding reins, therefore, must always act *unilaterally, and never simultaneously on both sides.* If this rein acts on one side its main effect is the *elimination of its action on the other side.* As soon as the horse has learnt to give on both hands it is useless to continue with the sliding reins.

When sliding reins are used to squeeze a horse into a certain position by mere force all real 'dressage' comes to an end. Such a procedure sooner or later unfailingly results in disobedience.

If the sliding reins are used in the proper manner, success should be apparent *within the first few minutes.* If not, it only proves that the rider does not know how to handle them, and in that case *he would do far better to discard them at once.*

THE WHIP

The riding-whip (cutting-whip) must be springy, and its upper end should be heavy enough to place its centre of gravity within the rider's hand. This allows it to be used freely, without the necessity of making sweeping movements with the hand, as is the case with a short stick or crop. Fig. 24, second from below, shows how the whip should be held.

The whip should be used with a short, smart, and determined tap just behind the girth. The horse should not at the same time be frightened by a whizzing noise.

If a tap with the whip is necessary, it should be an 'honest-to-goodness' smack and not a hesitating tickle, as if trying to find out 'what the horse is going to do about it'!

But the whip must never be used in temper and the rider should always have full control over the lightness or severeness of the punishment.

When mounting a horse with a whip it should always be carried in the left hand and not brandished about just in front of the animal's nose.

If the rider is handed a whip when mounted, it should be done in a manner that avoids making the horse nervous. Most horses hate the sight of a whip.

The whip is used:

On green horses, to make them understand the driving influences of legs and back-muscles. (See p. 72.)

On schooled or badly schooled horses if they hang heavy on the bit (see p. 108), or if they do not answer the driving legs (like the green horse); also if they are lazy and require a punishment.

When a horse does not respond, or not sufficiently, to the rider's legs he should receive a 'tactful reminder' in the shape of an instantaneous tap with the whip. This applies to the forward movement as well as to side-stepping. If, however, the tap comes too late, the horse does not associate the whip with the leg-action, and is only intimidated and frightened.

The inexperienced rider should never use the whip for punishment, because in most cases it will not be the horse who is to blame but his own lack of skill or his inability properly to judge and understand his mount's psychological constitution.

SPURS

A young rider should not be given spurs, because, not being able to control his legs, he would only tickle or perhaps even injure his horse with them. It is time enough to give a rider spurs when he has learnt to master his own limbs. Spurs are required to add emphasis to the leg action. If they are used too persistently, the horse gradually gets numb. The less the spurs are required the better. A horse defends himself against the spur by kicking at it with the hind legs (cow-kicking). Cow-kicking always indicates that the spur has not been used with the necessary emphasis, that the action was hesitating or that it lasted too long. A horse will never resent a quick, sharp prick at the instant we require something of him. If he cow-kicks at the spurs the rider should take this as a warning and realize that he is not applying the spurs correctly. The same is true of a horse which starts swishing and twisting his tail. Many horses constantly twist their tails because they are being tickled with spurs. And it often happens that the rider, when reminded of the fact by the instructor, answers: 'I haven't even touched him with the spurs'—the trouble being that he does not *feel* when his spurs are tickling his horse's sides. The rider must feel, and correctly feel, how and where his legs touch the horse's body. If he doesn't, he had better take off his spurs and set about acquiring this feel. (See p. 32.)

The spurs should be applied with a short sharp prick close behind the girth, the rider just bending his knee lightly. The toes must be lowered a fraction. Spur pricks without simultaneous leg- and back-muscle influences are useless.

Particular care and caution with the spurs must be observed with ticklish horses and mares in heat.

THE VOICE

An aid which the rider has always at his disposal is his voice. It can have an encouraging or a calming effect. The voice should be used in the same way as the spurs and the whip, with sympathy and understanding. A kind low voice has a calming effect, while a hard and shrill voice will upset a horse. There should never be shouting in the stables.

THE LUNGE

The lunge is a means of exercising a horse on foot; it is about twenty-five feet long, and is held in the left hand when lunging a horse 'on the left' and in the right hand when lunging 'on the right-hand' circle. The lunge can either be fastened to a cavesson or to the rings of the snaffle. The loose end of the lunge is held in the hand, forming a number of loops which should not hang down too far. The loops ought to be so arranged that the lunge can at any time be lengthened by 'paying out rope'.

The hand holding the lunge should be approximately at the height of the horse's mouth and should constantly keep the lunge taut. To lunge a horse with arms hanging down and the lunge dragging on the ground is just 'moving a horse', but does not deserve the expression 'lunging'.

Lunging is useful for first exercising a green horse. It is also valuable for correcting certain faults in a horse, for schooling over jumps, for horses with poor backs and loins,[1] for horses who have lost their spring under a rider, and, finally, for horses who must be exercised lightly as, e.g. after an illness.

On the lunge, the horse must show quiet, regular paces. Important items are the correct adjustment of the side reins and discretion in the simultaneous use of lunge, lunging whip, and voice. The last two to a certain extent replace the rider's back- and leg-influences, whereas the influences of the reins are represented by the active lunge and the passive side reins. The adjustment of these latter, as well as the use of whip and voice, demand a high degree of skill, experience, and concentration. The length of the side reins will probably have to be altered several times during the work. Lunging a horse is much more difficult than most people think.

[1] A rider who has not learned properly to follow the movement of the horse can never atone for this lack of knowledge by lunging his horse. A ruined or badly-mouthed horse can sometimes superficially, and for a short time, improve by being lunged, but he will soon relapse into his former condition if his rider cannot properly sit.

CAVALLETTIS—GROUNDBARS

Cavallettis are made of either railway sleepers or bars three metres long (ten feet), which are supported by cross-like sides. Cavallettis are used about 20 cm above the ground (8 to 10 inches). They can also be used at three different heights—10, 15, and 19 inches. The horse is ridden over them, at the walk or at the trot.

The advantages of cavalletti exercises are:

(1) That the horse will pay more attention to the ground, and will have to step higher. If the rider does not disturb the horse during these exercises, he will achieve the stretching forwards and downwards of the horse's head and neck and the relaxation of the muscles of the back.

The exercises can also be done on the lunge, without a rider.

One must not ask too much of a horse; especially a horse with an excitable nature, or one with a weak back. The bars should not be too easily dislodged, especially if the exercises are done in a ride, as then the distances are wrong for the next horse. This does more harm than good.

(2) That the rider can feel his own suppleness and his ability to adapt himself to the horse's movements. He must take care not to be behind the movement, and not to disturb the horse in the mouth and back. The rider closes his knees more firmly, and goes well into the movement of the horse.*

Cavallettis can be used successfully for horses with a very short back, to make them supple; and for horses which are spoiled, do not relax their back muscles and have no proper rhythm. †

* See forward seat on pages 34 and 35.

†Rhythm means the regular timing and equal length of the horse's steps and strides, within a definite tempo.

MAXIMUM SPREAD OF THE HORSE OVER A JUMP

Espartaco, Winner of the German Show Jumping Derby 1962. Nelson Pessoa up

THE LEVADE

PLATE I

THE INFLUENCE
OF THE LOWER
PART OF THE
RIDER'S BACK

(Compare drawings on pages 16, 17 and 117)

HORSE BEING LED
AT THE WALK

It is very instructive to watch a horse being led at a walk. A normally built animal will bring his hind legs about 8ins. forward of the hoof prints of the fore legs. It cannot, of course, be the object of 'collection' to increase this far-reaching flat gait. By 'collection' we want to put more load on to the hind-quarters, which requires an entirely different way of moving the legs. Their action must become higher or 'prouder', but at the same time the stride must needs become shorter

PLATE 2

Frau Rosemarie Springer on 'Brilliant'

VOLTE TO THE RIGHT AT THE TROT

Bent to the right, the horse steps forward and sideways. The right diagonal is about to step off

The Spanish Riding School, Vienna

Right shoulder-in at the trot. The diagonal pair of legs step simultaneously, the inside (right) hindleg steps into the same track as the outside (left) front leg. Horses bent to the right

PLATE 3

THE
BACK-MUSCLE
ACTION
(*see also Fig. 6, page 18*)

LOOSE BACK

BACK BRACED
at the middle trot

*Rittmeister Gerhard
on 'Fels'*

INCREASED BRACING
OF THE BACK
*at the halt from the
middle trot*

*Major Burkner
on 'Rosenkelch'*

PLATE 4

THE 'PASSAGE' (HAUTE ÉCOLE) OR 'SPANISH TROT'
CHIEF INSTRUCTOR MEIXNER OF THE SPANISH RIDING SCHOOL
OF VIENNA
Extreme collection at the trot

THE 'PIAFFE' (HAUTE ÉCOLE).   CHIEF INSTRUCTOR MEIXNER
Extreme collection at the trot on the spot

PLATE 5

VARIOUS TYPES OF THE TROT

RACING TROT

Photographing a horse at the trot should always be done so that the front leg, which is nearest to the photographer, is reaching out pointing well forward

EXTENDED TROT

Herr Willy Schultheiss, many times German Champion, four times winner of the German Dressage Derby

PASSAGE[1]
(*Haute École*)
Highest collection at the trot

[1]*Not to be confounded with the 'passage' in the English sense of the word, denoting a side movement or 'Travers'*

1st Lieut. Sandstrom (Sweden) on 'Sabel'

PLATE 6

VARIOUS TYPES OF THE TROT

WORKING TROT

Ordinary working trot on the aids without collection. Spanish Riding School, Vienna. Young remount during early training. Compare the weak muscular structure of this young horse with the fully muscled up trained school horse (Plate 1b)

COLLECTED TROT

Slightly more collected trot. Advanced remount of the Spanish Riding School, Vienna

PIAFFE

(*High School*)

Greatest collection, trot on the spot. The thoroughbred Arab entire Kanzler, Herr Eugen Kauffmann-Langenargen up

PLATE 7

VARIOUS
TYPES OF THE
CANTER

RACING GALLOP
(left)

The left fore will stretch
still more

MEDIUM CANTER

A little too short in
the neck

Frhr. von Langen
on 'Auer'

COLLECTED
CANTER

After having been stretched
the left fore is put down

Herr O. Loerke
on 'Artus'

PLATE 8

VARIOUS
TYPES OF THE
CANTER

WORKING CANTER
(left)
with loose reins, without
any collection

Frl. von Opel
on 'Arnim'

WORKING CANTER
at the aids, with slight
collection

Herr A. Staeck
on 'Ingo'

PIROUETTE
(left)
(High School)
Highest collection at
the canter

Chief Instructor W. Zrust,
Spanish Riding School,
Vienna

PLATE 9

CANTER
LEFT
straight ahead

Major Burkner

CANTER
LEFT
in a turn

Frhr. von Langen

PLATE 10

ıst LIEUT. SAHLA ON 'WOTAN'

PLATE 11

SHOW JUMPING WORLD CHAMPION 1956, 1960 RAIMONDO
D'INZEO, ITALY, WITH HIS WELL KNOWN 'MERANO' IN THE BEST
ITALIAN STYLE TAKING THE IRISH BANK IN AACHEN

PLATE 12

Frhr. v. Langen

Lieut. Müseler

Major Ricci (Italy)

THE SEAT OVER A JUMP

Correct harmony, rider following the movement, good knee grip, lower legs not flopping, steady hands, the horses stretch their necks, the bent arms allow of further giving should it be necessary at any moment

PLATE 13

Good position of the rider advancing his weight without getting too far out of the saddle, low hands, contact with the horse's mouth, looking straight ahead and correct position of leg and feet. Tarlatane with Commandant Fresson, France, up

Rider behind the movement, is being dragged along by the horse and interferes with his mouth

Rider more behind the movement and inconveniencing the horse still more

PLATE 14

Lengthening of arm and wrist gives the horse maximum stretch of neck and back (Pascule). Alpenmarchen with Major von Ziegner up

Rider behind the movement; lands safely by giving his mount absolute freedom of neck. Monte Rosa with Sepp von Radowitz up

If your horse pecks badly grip tight with your knees and don't interfere with your hands. The animal will try his best to extricate itself. Vagant with Reiner Klimke up

PLATE 15

Rittm. v. Barnckow

HIGH JUMP

*No exaggeration!
Splendid example! A
rather steep jump, be-
cause the horse has run
up too close to obstacle.
Had the rider remained
in the saddle he would
have been hopelessly
left behind. His effort
resulted in a clean
jump!*

*Cmdr. Chamberlain
(U.S.A.)*

JUMP FROM
A BANK

*At a downward jump
it is easier to follow
the movement, at the
same time it shows
clearly whether the
rider has nerve*

PLATE 16